Lindergaff Books

San Francisco

The Dancing Gourmet

Recipes to Keep You on Your Toes!

Linda Hymes

with photography by Derek Gaffney

Sketches on pp.38, 62 copyright ©2002 Alan Kluckow.
Original paintings on pages 11,20, 111 copyright 2002 © by Alan Kluckow, photographed by Derek Gaffney.
All photography in this book taken by Derek Gaffney except the following black & white photos:
pp. 6, 12,70,88, 116 - copyright ©2002 Jennifer W. Lester.
p. 46 copyright ©2002 Jeffrey C. Brown/INCOGNITO.
pp. 13, 31, 47, 71, 89, 117 - copyright ©2002 Christopher Jean-Richard.
Photograph on page 88 of George Balanchine's **The Nutcracker™** , choreography by George Balanchine ©The George Balanchine Trust.
Photograph on page 116 of **Tarantella**, choreography by George Balanchine ©The George Balanchine Trust.

A portion of the proceeds of this book will be donated to the Dancing Gourmet fund.
Thank you for supporting the arts.

Cover page lettering for "The Dancing Gourmet" and logo drawn by artist Tony Chiofolo.

Design and Food Styling by Linda Hymes

Cover photo by Derek Gaffney
Special thanks to Marcello Angelini and Tulsa Ballet Theatre for generously donating studio time and costumes.
Cover tutu designed by Carl Michel

Published in 2002 by Lindergaff Books
Lindergaff Books
643 Carolina St.
San Francisco, California 94107
www.dancinggourmet.com

Library of Congress Cataloging-in Publication Data
Hymes, Linda.
    The Dancing Gourmet: Recipes to keep you on your toes!/Linda Hymes: photographs by Derek Gaffney
    and others; photo styling by Linda Hymes.
        p.   cm.
    ISBN 0-9719782-0-4
    1. Cookery, General   2. Ballet   I.Hymes, Linda.   II. Title.
    2002091154

PRINTED IN HONG KONG

First Edition
10 9 8 7 6 5 4 3 2 1

For extra copies of this book and information about Lindergaff Books, please visit our website at **http://www.dancinggourmet.com**
or call us at 1(866) NUTCRACKER (1-866-688-2722).

Contents

Guide to using the recipes in this book:

The recipes in The Dancing Gourmet are designed to incorporate highly flavorful and naturally nutritious foods that require little in the way of heavy sauces or fats to make them delicious and satisfying. Whether you are trying to lose weight or just maintain a healthful approach to eating, these recipes will make exciting additions to your culinary repertoire. Keep in mind the following tips for the best results:

1. Buy the best. The success of recipes is dependent on the correct measurements of the highest quality ingredients. Dancers will often try on twenty different pointe shoes before choosing one pair for a performance, based on how they look and feel on their feet. If a certain ballet requires a lot of jumping, a softer shoe will be chosen so the impact on the stage will be soundless, yet a role with many turns may merit a shoe with stiffer shanks and very flat tip. Take the same care in choosing your food. An avocado which will be sliced and presented with little adornment, as in the shrimp cocktail recipe, needs to be perfectly ripe with no imperfections. A tomato which has attained a vibrant vermillion will taste better than an unripe one with a greenish pallor. Pick a firm intensely purple eggplant and grill it for the Thai eggplant salad rather than buying the limp bruised arugula displayed just because the chicken salad with blackberry dressing looked so appetizing. Quite often I go to the market with the intention of cooking one menu and return home with grocery bags full of ingredients for completely different dishes, because what was freshest at the store was not what I had in mind. I might go in thinking poached salmon, and upon taking a quick glance at the fish display turn right around and head for the meat. In other words, be flexible and buy the best you can afford. It is better to use the freshest plump chicken as the principal role in a recipe than buying a bargain cut of inferior quality beef. If you are concerned about cost, make something deliciously unusual but still affordable-- your guests will be equally tempted by an exotic Moroccan chicken tagine with preserved lemon as they will with the pricier Chilean sea bass wrapped in pancetta.
2. Large eggs should be used wherever a recipe calls for eggs.
3. Pepper should be freshly ground black unless otherwise indicated.
4. It is assumed that all meats, poultry, fruits and vegetables will be washed and dried before cooking.
5. Fresh herbs should be used unless otherwise stated. Most of the recipes in this book call for fresh herbs because they are an integral part of the taste and texture of the dish. Dried herbs should only be substituted where the herbs are used as part of sauces. Never use dried where a recipe calls for fresh coriander or cilantro-- the taste is very different and is better omitted altogether.
6. Always measure and prepare ingredients before you begin cooking. This is called *mise en place* and helps greatly when you are making several different dishes that need to be served at the same time.
7. Dishes that call for salt and pepper to taste should be added at the end of cooking time, when you can best judge the seasoning. Keep in mind that sauces that are simmered or cooked slowly tend to concentrate their flavors over time. Seasoning too early may make a dish taste too salty or peppery by the time it has finished cooking. Remember that you can always add more if need be but a French onion soup that is too salty is beyond repair.
8. Whenever possible, try to grind dried herbs just before you use them in a recipe. If they are bought whole and in small quantities, they will still be fresh when called upon for a recipe, rather than a bulk supply, which by the time you have gotten your money's worth, your herbs power has long since faded. Buy fresh and toast lightly in a dry pan before using to bring out the flavor.

Non-cooks think it is silly to invest two hours work into two minutes enjoyment, but if cooking is evanescent, so is the ballet.

- Julia Child

Introduction

Long before I hung up my pointe shoes I realized as much as I loved to dance, what I really lived for was to eat. The aroma of freshly brewed coffee enticed me out of bed in the morning and the thought of lunch pushed me through grand allegro combinations at the end of morning class. I must admit too, that more than once as I bowed to an audience after a performance I was thinking about what I was going to make for dinner. As rewarding as the applause was, the real treat was food, and lots of it!

I suppose the making of two careers began in New York City in my tiny upper west side kitchen, making dinner on the single burner hot plate I called my stove. I mashed tomatoes into a thick purée while dutifully rotating my legs in semi-circular patterns on the floor, devoting as much concentration to loosening my hips from their sockets as the tomato flesh from its skin. The making of dinner was a ritual to be savored and never rushed, a reward for all the day's energy burned. Maybe it was the pressure to stay thin that made each bite taste so good. Balanchine once said dancers are among the few people in this world who can have their cake and eat it too. I was determined to be one of those few.

Throughout my training at the School of American Ballet, teachers illustrated their corrections with similes and metaphors; one must land from a jump softly like a pouncing cat and lift the body from the center as if hanging from a single thread. Of course, the most poignant images were those that also appealed to my taste buds: balonés juicy like squeezing fresh lemons, fondues that melt like butter, developpés with the hip turned out enough to serve a glass of champagne on the heel. By the end of warm-up I'd sweated myself into quite an imaginary feast! As much as I enjoyed a good meal, I was destined to practice a dietary regime which would not impinge on my career. Fortunately this kind of caloric fantasy improved my technique without expanding my waistline. The kitchen was where my days began and ended, where I practiced my ronds de jambe à terre while waiting for the kettle to boil.

Years later, in the more relaxed atmosphere of company class, gastronomic revelries were shared with fellow dancers. I was blessed to be employed among artists with similar passions, and discussions of the finer points of roasting a chicken or baking brie often took place while stretching at the barre or preparing for a pirouette. On occasion, we could even do our required exercises with the utmost of concentration, jeté across the room and continue discussing dessert without missing a beat! Many a night was spent bringing those conversations to life cooking in each other's kitchen. In fact, relaxing after a performance with a home-cooked meal and good wine with fellow dancers and friends remains one of my most treasured memories of my career.

Contrary to popular belief, professional ballet dancers love and eat real food and do not exist on rations of rice cakes and lettuce. A ballerina, like a professional athlete, requires a healthy balanced diet to produce the necessary energy to be in peak condition. Getting through Concerto Barocco requires a lot more than just technique and inspiration!

Everyone can benefit from a dancer's approach to food. Fortunately, learning to eat like a dancer doesn't take nearly the discipline of becoming one. Ballet is not instant art. Becoming a dancer takes long hours at the barre each day doing the same steps over and over again until movements that are inherently unnatural become automatic. This is what we call muscle memory. The process of training the body by repetition of movement is extremely important. The last thing a ballerina wants to think about on stage is how to do a step! Likewise you can train yourself so that what you eat becomes instinctual. Unlike classical ballet, good eating habits do not require any great discipline, just the proper knowledge and a little practice.

This is not a diet cookbook. I don't diet and I honestly don't know many professional dancers who do. Dancers are thin because they get plenty of exercise and eat properly. If there is a secret to looking like a ballerina, it's not what you eat; it's simply the amount and how you prepare your food. It's about balance. The recipes in this book have helped me to keep that balance so that a hefty piece of chocolate cake or a juicy cheeseburger now and then don't show.

This book is a compilation of a career of cooking, eating, dancing and traveling. There are delicious recipes from all over the world that are great for everyday meals as well as entertaining, illustrated with vibrant color photographs. All the recipes use fresh ingredients, fragrant spices and are simple to prepare. Let your taste buds dance for joy and please support the arts.

assemblé

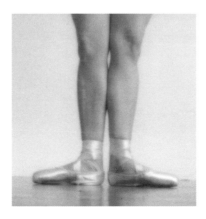

First

Starting at the Barre...Appetizers and Small Plates

Warm up to dinner with these little plates that flex the taste buds and wake up your stomach muscles- without stretching your thighs! These light and tasty starters make tempting overtures for entertaining. They can also be extended to make small meals by themselves, to be enjoyed on their own or with cocktails. With an emphasis on taste rather than quantity, small plates are as satisfying to the eye as the palate. The following recipes fit the bill in fat and calories and especially taste.

gravlax with marinated cucumbers
classic scallop ceviche
quick salsa
goi cuon (vietnamese summer rolls)
shrimp cocktail with avocado and green apple
chicken saté
avocado hummus
smoky white bean baba ghanoosh
sautéed wild mushrooms with pan-fried polenta squares
spanikopita divas
basic steps to sushi
delicate sesame chicken dumplings
crostini with pesto and slow roasted tomatoes
edamame
tuna tartare

gravlax

Making gravlax at home is so easy you'll never buy expensive and salty packaged lox again. Bite size open-faced sandwiches make elegant hors d'oeuvres, topped with a few capers or a spoonful of mustard sauce. Serve on pumpernickel bread with marinated cucumbers. Leftover gravlax is delicious for Sunday brunch on fresh bagels with cream cheese.

Serves 8

Allow 48 hours marinating time before serving.

1 lb. fresh salmon fillet, with skin, cut into 2 pieces
3 tablespoons coarse sea salt
1/3 cup sugar
1 bunch fresh dill, coarsely chopped
1 tablespoon mixed white and black peppercorns, crushed
1 tablespoon juniper berries, crushed

Rinse and dry salmon. Mix remaining curing ingredients together. Pack curing mixture all over salmon then sandwich fillets together. Wrap tightly in plastic wrap then again in tin foil. Place in a small casserole and weigh down with a brick or gallon of milk. Marinate in refrigerator 2 full days, turning fish over every 12 hours. Drain off any liquid that accumulates in the dish.
To serve: Unwrap fillets and scrape off curing mixture. Cut skin off and slice very thinly. Garnish with lemon slices, fresh dill sprigs, marinated cucumbers, sauces, and pumpernickel bread.

horseradish sauce

½ cup non-fat plain yoghurt
1 ½ teaspoons finely grated fresh horseradish
freshly ground white pepper to taste

Place yogurt in a strainer lined with 2-3 paper towels and let liquid drain 1 hour. Scoop thickened yogurt into a small bowl. Add horseradish and pepper. Stir and chill until ready to serve.

traditional gravlax sauce

Just a drizzle of this traditional vinaigrette nicely sets off the sweetness of sugar-cured salmon.

2 tablespoons white wine vinegar
2 tablespoons dijon mustard
1 egg yolk
1 tablespoon sugar
¼ teaspoon salt
¼ teaspoon dill weed
freshly ground white pepper to taste
5 tablespoons vegetable oil

Combine all ingredients except oil in a medium bowl. Add vegetable oil in a slow steady stream while whisking constantly and continue whisking until sauce thickens. Cover with plastic until ready to serve.

brown sugar sauce

¼ cup brown mustard
¼ cup light brown sugar
1 tablespoon fresh chopped dill

Combine all ingredients and mix well. Chill until ready to serve.

marinated cucumbers

The sweet crunch of thinly sliced cucumbers complements gravlax which has been cured with more sugar than salt. Make them shortly before you plan to serve them, as they tend to get soft the longer they sit in the marinade. These cucumbers also taste great mixed into green salads with creamy dill or honey mustard dressing.

1/3 cup white vinegar
1/3 cup water
¾ tablespoon sugar
¼ teaspoon salt
freshly ground white pepper to taste
1 large cucumber, sliced paper thin

Combine all ingredients except cucumbers in a medium bowl and mix well. Stir in sliced cucumbers. Cover and chill for 1 hour before serving.

gravlax with marinated cucumbers

classic scallop ceviche

This popular Mexican starter uses fresh bay scallops that are "cooked" by the acidity in the lime juice. Use only the freshest ingredients and chill fish until opaque. Shrimp, cubed swordfish, flounder or other white fish can be substituted for the scallops.

Serves 4

1 lb. fresh large sea scallops
½ cup freshly squeezed lime juice
¼ cup freshly squeezed lemon juice
½ red onion, thinly sliced
½ jalapeno, seeded and sliced
2-3 drops hot red pepper sauce
2 scallions, finely chopped
2 ripe roma tomatoes, seeded and chopped
1 tablespoon extra-virgin olive oil
¼ cup fresh cilantro leaves, finely chopped
freshly ground black pepper

Rinse scallops and slice in half widthwise. Place in a bowl small enough so scallops will be completely covered with juices, red onion, jalapeno, and a drop or two of red pepper sauce. Cover with plastic and chill 3 hours. Drain liquid from fish and toss gently with remaining ingredients. Serve in chilled glass bowls.

quick salsa

This is a variation on a salsa recipe I scribbled on a napkin in a southwestern restaurant in Phoenix. It is more sweet than spicy, and perfect with margaritas after a show.

Makes about 3 cups

2 large ripe tomatoes, seeded and quartered
1 green pepper, seeded and diced
4 green onions, trimmed and sliced
1 jalapeno pepper, seeded
½ cup fresh cilantro leaves, chopped
1 tablespoon sugar
6 tablespoons tomato paste
½ teaspoon salt
1/3 - 2/3 cups water, depending on consistency desired

Combine tomatoes, green pepper, scallions, and jalapeno in the bowl of a food processor and pulse until chopped. Add remaining ingredients and pulse a few more times, just until mixed. (Or make by hand: finely chop tomatoes, green pepper, scallions and jalapeno. Add remaining ingredients and stir well to mix.)
Transfer to a serving bowl and cover with plastic wrap. Let stand one hour. Stir again and serve with fat-free baked tortilla chips.

goi cuon

(vietnamese summerrolls with pork and shrimp)

When I danced in Ohio, our main season took place when most other companies were laid-off. From June through August, we were booked in a series of free outdoor performances, as a part of northeastern Ohio's summer arts festival. The stage was a full size moveable theatre, complete with scaffolding for lights, upstage wings and a cross-over for entrances and exits. Our dressing rooms were large tents with folding chairs and tables and since we normally rehearsed from noon up to one hour before the performance, some of the dancers would bring small coolers with food and munch while they put on their makeup. I loved to make these summerrolls because they are light and just enough to carry me through a show.

The fillings can be varied to include tofu or strips of chicken and are easy to make once you get used to working with the rice paper rounds. Serve immediately or cover with a damp cloth in the refrigerator for up to 2 hours.

4 oz. rice vermicelli
1 teaspoon vegetable oil
1 lb. lean pork tenderloin, trimmed of fat and cut into thin strips
½ lb. medium shrimp, shelled and cleaned
freshly ground black pepper
1 medium carrot, shredded
5 oz. mesclun or baby greens
10 oz. fresh mung bean sprouts
2 oz. fresh mint leaves
2 oz. fresh cilantro leaves
12 rounds rice paper (banh trang)

dipping sauce:
½ cup hoisin sauce
1 tablespoon chili garlic sauce
1 tablespoon shredded carrots
2 tablespoons chopped unsalted peanuts

Place dried rice vermicelli in a bowl and pour hot water to cover. Let soften about 30 minutes, until noodles are done, then drain water and spread noodles on a paper towel to remove excess moisture. Set aside.

Heat oil in a non-stick wok or frying pan over high heat. Sprinkle pork and shrimp with freshly ground pepper. Add pork strips and shrimp and sauté just until they lose their pink color, about 3 minutes. Remove from heat.

Line up rice vermicelli, pork, shrimp, shredded carrot, mesclun, bean sprouts, mint, and cilantro leaves so they are ready for filling banh trang.

Fill a bowl large enough in which to dip the rice paper rounds (banh trang) without having to bend them (or fill the sink about 2 inches deep with hot water). Dip one round rice paper at a time for a few seconds, then place on a damp cloth. Cover with another cloth and let round soften, about 10 seconds. Take cloth off top and fill center of round with a few strips pork, a couple of shrimp, and a tablespoon or two each of carrots, bean sprouts, mint, and cilantro leaves.

Fold one end of rice paper over fillings then roll tightly into a cylinder. Repeat with remaining banh trang and fillings.

Cut each summerroll in half and arrange on a plate. Make dipping sauce by topping hoisin sauce in a small bowl with garlic sauce, carrots, and chopped peanuts.

Mix together mayonnaise and ketchup with a fork. Stir in vodka and pepper. Alternate shrimp, sliced avocado and green apple on a plate and serve with mayonnaise dip.

chicken saté

These slender skewers sizzling with Thai spices will win rave reviews from your guests. Freeze skewered and marinated raw chicken ahead of time then thaw on the day you plan to serve them. They only take a few minutes to cook under a hot broiler, just remember to cover wooden skewer handles with aluminum foil to prevent them from burning. This recipe also tastes great made with shrimp.

Serves 6-8 as an appetizer

2 teaspoons fennel seeds
1 tablespoon whole coriander seeds
2 teaspoons dried or 1 tablespoon fresh finely minced lemongrass
½ teaspoon ground turmeric
2 teaspoons palm or light brown sugar
¼ teaspoon salt
2 tablespoons low-sodium or regular soy sauce
1 tablespoon sesame oil
2 tablespoons fresh lime juice
4 large boneless and skinless chicken breasts or 2 lbs. chicken tenders, trimmed of fat

12-15 wooden, bamboo or metal skewers
vegetable oil cooking spray

In a small heavy skillet, toast fennel and coriander seeds over medium heat until a few shades darker. Grind in a small food processor, spice grinder or mortar and pestle to a powder, then mix with lemongrass, turmeric, palm or brown sugar, and salt. Whisk in soy sauce, sesame oil, and lime juice.
Cut cleaned and trimmed chicken into strips (about 4 pieces per breast of chicken) and skewer on metal or wooden sticks. Line skewers close together on a large platter and spread marinade over top, turning to coat all over. Cover platter with plastic wrap and refrigerate at least 2 hours (or freeze up to a week in advance). Preheat broiler. If using wooden skewers, cover ends with tin foil to prevent burning. Spray skewers lightly with vegetable oil spray and broil 4 minutes on each side. Serve immediately.

shrimp cocktail with avocado and green apple

Pollyana Ribiero of the Boston Ballet gave me the idea for this recipe, recommending it for parties since it is so easy to make. I also like to serve it as an hors d'oeuvre, skewered in bite-size pieces on toothpicks with the sauce in a bowl for dipping.

Serves 4

½ cup light mayonnaise
3 tablespoons ketchup
1 teaspoon vodka or red wine
white pepper
16 jumbo shrimp, cleaned, cooked and peeled with the tails left on
1 large ripe avocado, peeled and sliced
1 large tart green apple, sliced

chicken saté

avocado hummus

Non-fat yoghurt makes this quick and easy spread smooth and creamy without the oil that drowns most deli versions. Use as a dip for crudité, with triangles of pita bread or as a sandwich spread with alfalpha sprouts.

Makes about 2 cups

2 (15oz.) cans chick peas
3 cloves garlic, finely minced
3- 4 tablespoons fresh lemon juice
3 tablespoons tahini
¼ - ½ teaspoon salt, to taste
½ teaspoon ground cumin
1/8 teaspoon garam masala, optional
½ cup non-fat plain yoghurt
1 ripe avocado, peeled and pitted

Drain beans and rinse in a colander until water runs clear. Purée beans with garlic in a blender or food processor. Add remaining ingredients and blend until thick and smooth. Add more salt or lemon juice if desired. Transfer to a bowl, cover, and chill until ready to serve. Keeps several days in the refrigerator.

smoky white bean baba ganoosh

Makes about 2 cups

1 large eggplant
olive oil cooking spray
1- 2 cloves garlic, chopped
1 (15½ oz.) can cannellini (white kidney) beans
2 tablespoons non-fat plain yoghurt
2 tablespoons tahini
1 tablespoon fresh lemon juice
salt and pepper

Cut the stem end off the eggplant and cut in half lengthwise. Spray lightly with olive oil spray on both sides and place skin-sides down on a baking sheet. Broil under high heat until skin becomes soft, wrinkled and charred, about 5-10 minutes. Turn over and broil 2-3 minutes more just to lightly char the flesh, being careful not to burn the flesh of the eggplant. Remove from heat, place on a dish, and set aside.
When eggplant has cooled, scoop out flesh and discard skin. Place flesh in the bowl of a food processor or blender with garlic and pulse a few times to mash. Add cannellini beans, yoghurt, tahini, lemon juice, salt, and freshly ground pepper to taste. Pulse a few times, then process just to a paste, about 10 seconds. Transfer to a small bowl, cover, and chill. Serve with triangles of fresh pita bread.

sautéed wild mushrooms
with pan-fried polenta squares

Dancing in Italy exposed me not only to fabulous pasta but also to a simple appetizer from Tuscany that has since become one of my favorites. Polenta is extremely versatile and has little or no fat per serving. If you can't find fresh wild mushrooms all white mushrooms can be used instead.

Serves 4-6

1 lb. mixed wild mushrooms, cleaned and sliced (chanterelle, shiitake, porcini, or portobello)
2 teaspoons olive oil
2 cloves garlic, minced
¼ cup dry white wine
3 sprigs fresh thyme or 1 teaspoon dried
2 tablespoons fresh italian parsley, chopped
¼ teaspoon salt
freshly ground black pepper to taste
16 oz. prepared polenta, cut in ½ inch thick slices
olive or vegetable oil flavored cooking spray
fresh thyme sprigs for garnish

Heat olive oil in a large skillet over medium-high heat. Sauté garlic and mushrooms until they begin to give off their liquid, about 5 minutes. Add thyme and white wine and cook until liquid in pan evaporates. Season with salt and pepper and sprinkle parsley over mushrooms. Keep warm.
Spray another large skillet with oil cooking spray. Fry sliced polenta in a single layer on each side until edges turn golden. Serve topped with mushrooms and a sprig of fresh thyme.

spanikopita divas

I created these little Greek appetizers after trying spinach pie, or spanikopita, at a little taverna in the Plakka in Athens. Individually wrapping them in phyllo makes for easy finger food.

Makes approx. 30 little pastries

10 oz. fresh spinach, roughly chopped
½ cup red onion, finely chopped
2 teaspoons extra-virgin olive oil
3 tablespoons pine nuts, roughly chopped
¾ cup reduced-fat feta cheese, crumbled
¼ cup low-fat cottage cheese
2 tablespoons grated parmesan cheese
1 ½ teaspoons fresh chopped herbs (dill, mint or oregano)
1 tablespoon lemon juice
2 egg whites
salt and freshly ground black pepper to taste
12 oz. frozen phyllo dough, thawed
1 egg, mixed with 2 tablespoons water
¼ cup butter, melted

Preheat oven to 350 degrees.
Place spinach in a colander and rinse with water. Place rinsed spinach in a pot and place over high heat. The water left on the leaves should be enough to steam the spinach. Cook just until leaves wilt, then remove from heat and drain in a colander, pressing down with a paper towel to remove excess moisture.
Sauté onions in olive oil until soft, about 2 minutes, then add pine nuts and cook 1 minute more. Transfer to a bowl with the cheeses, herbs, lemon juice, and egg whites. Season with salt and freshly ground black pepper. Mix well.
Lay two sheets of phyllo dough on top of each other and brush lightly with egg mixture. Cut sheet into 5 strips, each about 3 x13 inches. Spoon 1 tablespoon filling at one end of each strip and fold edge of phyllo over filling into a triangle, then keep folding triangle over like a flag to the end of the strip.
Repeat with remaining phyllo and filling, then place pies onto a non-stick baking sheet. Brush top of each pie with melted butter. Bake 20 minutes, or until edges turn golden. Serve warm.

spanikopita divas

basic steps to sushi

Sushi is the perfect snack, starter or light meal to keep you looking like a ballerina. It is light and healthy but tasty and filling. Making sushi maki rolls at home is surprisingly simple, you just need the right ingredients. Only use raw fish if you can get sushi-grade quality. Even without raw fish, the fillings you can use are limitless. Try cooked fish such as shrimp or salmon with slivered green onion, or make your own "unagi" using slices of warm teriyaki-grilled trout. Cooked salmon and spinach, grilled teriyaki chicken with pineapple-- anything goes with rice! Do not use long grain rice as it lacks the glutinous texture and won't stick to the nori sheets. Bamboo rolling mats and short grain rice are inexpensive and available at Asian markets and better groceries.

cooked sushi rice (sushi can also be made with glutinous brown sushi rice or black sweet rice)
sushi vinegar
nori sheets (seaweed sushi roll wrappers)
wasabi paste (Japanese horseradish paste)
low-sodium or regular soy sauce
fillings of your choice (suggestions following)

sushi rice

Makes approximately 3 1/3 cups prepared rice, or enough for 8 maki rolls

½ cup cooked rice per 6 piece roll
1 ¼ cups white short grain glutinous rice
1 ¾ cups water

Rinse rice in a colander in several changes of water. Drain, then place in a medium size pot. Add 1 ¾ cups water. Bring to a boil and stir rice once or twice then reduce heat to low and cook approximately 12-15 minutes or until rice is tender, adding a little water to pot if necessary to prevent sticking. Remove from heat and let stand covered for 10 minutes then transfer to a large wooden or glass bowl.

Note: Rice must be barely warm or at room temperature. If the rice is too hot, the nori will break apart and cold rice will not stick. Let fresh cooked rice cool until just warm on your fingers and if your rice has been made ahead of time, place it in the microwave for a minute or two until just warm.

sushi vinegar

2 ½ tablespoons rice vinegar
½ teaspoon granulated sugar
¼ teaspoon salt

Place ingredients in a small saucepan and bring to a boil over high heat. Cook 1 minute then remove from heat. Let cool to room temperature. Sprinkle seasoned vinegar over warm rice and mix thoroughly with a wooden spoon.

tomago (sweetened egg omelet)

Makes 2 omelets

4 eggs
2 teaspoons granulated sugar
¼ teaspoon soy sauce
2 teaspoons cornstarch, dissolved in 2 teaspoons water

Whisk ingredients together then pour through a fine sieve to smooth out the mixture. Spray a small non-stick skillet or omelet pan with vegetable oil and place over medium-high heat. Pan is hot enough when drops of water sizzle and quickly evaporate. Pour the egg mixture into heated pan and cook 10 seconds, then flip half over onto other half and cook over low heat just until set, about 2 minutes. Slide omelet onto wax paper to cool, then cut into 1 inch thick strips. Set aside until ready to assemble maki rolls.

fillings:
blanched or raw julienned carrots and string beans
steamed spinach with a drop of sesame oil and toasted sesame seeds
crabmeat with cucumber and avocado
cooked shrimp, salmon, lobster, crab, scallop, trout, tuna, or smoked nova salmon with avocado with green onion
shiitake mushrooms and pickled gourd
grilled chicken with red bell pepper strips
pickled ginger, cabbage or beet
tomago with caviar
red bell pepper, blanched carrot, and string beans

tools:
one bamboo rolling mat and a large flat wooden spoon

The Basic Steps to assembling maki rolls:

On a flat surface, lay one sheet of nori on bamboo mat. (Cover your bamboo mat with a sheet of plastic wrap before you use it for easy cleaning.) Dab a little wasabi paste in the middle, then spread rice over nori with a large wooden spoon, leaving about an inch margin on the bottom. Lay desired fillings across margin, then carefully tuck the edge of the nori sheet over the fillings and continue rolling into a tight cylinder, pressing gently with the bamboo mat to make an even roll. Enclose finished maki roll in the bamboo mat and squeeze enclosed roll gently so the fillings and rice are tightly packed. Cut roll with a sharp serrated knife into 6 pieces. Repeat with remaining nori sheets. Arrange maki on a platter and garnish with pickled ginger slices and dipping sauce made of 1 teaspoon prepared wasabi to 1/3 cup soy sauce.

delicate sesame chicken dumplings

Serves 6-8

1 scallion
2 shallots
1 inch piece fresh ginger
1 clove garlic
¼ teaspoon chile sauce or finely chopped hot chile
½ teaspoon sesame oil
¾ lb. chicken tenderloins or breasts
2 tablespoons fresh coriander leaves
1 egg, beaten with 1 tablespoon water
1 lb. package wonton wrappers

low-sodium soy sauce
sesame oil
fresh chopped coriander leaves for garnish

Place scallion, shallots, ginger, and garlic in the bowl of a food processor and pulse a few times to chop finely. Add sesame oil, chile sauce, and chicken and process until chicken is ground. Add coriander leaves and pulse a few more times to chop. Transfer ground chicken to a bowl. Cover wonton wrappers with a damp cloth to prevent them from drying out. Working with one wrapper at a time, brush lightly with the egg mixture. Place a generous teaspoon of chicken in the center of the wonton, then place another wrapper over top, so it fits evenly over edges.

Gently press edges to seal, smoothing out from the center to remove any bubbles and make sure wonton edges are sticking together. Set finished wonton on a piece of wax paper and cover with a barely damp cloth. Repeat with remaining wontons.(They can be frozen uncooked at this point and will keep several weeks. When you are ready to cook them, slide them frozen into the boiling water and keep at a low boil 6-8 minutes until cooked through.)

Bring a large pot of water to a boil. Gently slide a few dumplings in at a time, stirring water very gently to prevent them from sticking together. Cook 3-4 minutes, or until dumplings rise to the top of the water. Remove with a slotted spatula and place on a heated plate to keep warm.

Serve 4-5 dumplings per person, drizzled with
½ teaspoon sesame oil and a few drops of soy sauce.

crostini with pesto and slow roasted tomatoes

4 ciabatta rolls or 1 loaf ciabatta bread, cut into ½ inch slices
1 medium red onion, sliced thinly
4 ripe tomatoes, thinly sliced crosswise
2 cloves garlic, finely minced
2 teaspoons extra-virgin olive oil, plus extra for drizzling over tops of crostini
salt and freshly ground black pepper
1 recipe pesto

Preheat oven to 350 degrees.
Place tomato and red onion slices on a large baking sheet. Scatter minced garlic over tops and season with salt and pepper. Drizzle top with 2 teaspoons olive oil. Bake 15 minutes, then reduce heat to 300 degrees and bake another 15 minutes, until tomatoes are soft and onion is nicely browned. Remove from oven and turn heat to broil. Brush ciabatta slices with a little olive oil and place on another baking sheet. Toast slices lightly in oven, then transfer to a serving tray. Top half the toasts with roasted tomatoes and onions and the other half with pesto. Drizzle a little oil over tops and serve immediately.

basil and italian parsley pesto

1 large bunch fresh basil leaves, about 2 cups loosely packed
½ cup loosely packed flat-leaf parsley
¼ cup extra-virgin olive oil
2 cloves garlic, crushed
¼ cup shredded parmesan or romano cheese
¼ cup pine nuts
salt and pepper to taste

Place pine nuts and garlic in a small food processor and pulse to chop roughly. Add remaining ingredients and process to a paste. Pesto will stay fresh several days covered tightly in the refrigerator.

edamame

Salted boiled soy beans are great for nibbling with cocktails and much healthier than chips or nuts. Find Japanese edamame in the frozen section of Asian markets and some better groceries and keep in your freezer for unexpected company.

Serves 4-6 as a starter

1 lb. bag fresh or frozen soybeans
coarse salt

Bring a large pot of salted water to a rapid boil and add soybeans. Cook about 5 minutes for fresh beans or until beans are tender (9 minutes for frozen beans). Drain and refresh with cold water. Sprinkle lightly with coarse salt and serve in a large bowl with small plates on the side for the empty pods.

tuna tartare

Unlike heavy beef tartare served with the usual trimmings of egg and capers, this lighter east-west version is made with sashimi-grade tuna, crisp cucumbers, and tomatoes, and served on colorful prawn crackers (also called shrimp chips). Prawn crackers taste best freshly made, which is what I like to do, because people always get a kick out of watching the little plastic-looking disks puff up into crunchy chips. Heat peanut oil in a wok to 375 degrees and add a few chips at a time, then remove with a slotted spoon or wire spider and drain on paper towels. Assemble just before serving so the chips don't become soggy.

Makes about 25

8 oz. sashimi-grade tuna, cut in small cubes
2 scallions, finely chopped
1/3 cup finely diced cucumber
¼ cup fresh cilantro leaves, finely chopped
2 tablespoons finely chopped tomato
2 tablespoons soy sauce
1 tablespoon spicy sesame oil
2 tablespoons rice vinegar
3-4 drops hot red pepper sauce

approx. 25-30 prawn crackers
¼ cup unsalted peanuts, chopped

Combine tuna, scallions, cilantro, cucumber, tomato, soy sauce, sesame oils, rice vinegar, and a few drops of hot red pepper sauce in a medium bowl. Mix well and spoon onto prepared prawn crackers. Top with a few chopped peanuts and serve immediately.

If you are trying to get a jump on preparation before your guests come, you can make the tartare in three parts. Fry up the prawn crackers a day ahead of time and store in a tight container. On the day you plan to serve the tartare combine the soy sauce, sesame oil, rice vinegar, and tabasco in a small bowl and cover with plastic. Place the chopped tuna, scallions, cucumber, cilantro, and tomato in a bowl then mix with soy sauce mixture just before serving.

tuna tartare

penchée

Second

Pas de Soupe

Slowly simmered on the stove, a steaming bowl of soup is the ultimate comfort food, an adagio of flavors melding together into a wholesome restorative brew. Soup requires little attention as it cooks, allowing time for a soak in the tub or an unwinding glass of wine. Whether chilled and sipped as easy Spanish gazpacho, or a nurturing broth of Asian noodles with tasty diminutive pork balls, these versatile recipes can be dressed into formal first courses or left casual for easy lunches and light dinners.

gazpacho andaluz
sweet corn and coconut egg drop soup
saratoga sweet potato and ginger purée
portobello soup with rosemary
french onion soup gratinée
udon with gingered pork balls
asian noodle soup with grilled chicken
basic chicken soup elixir
provençal potage of white bean and potato
curried pumpkin soup
easy split pea soup

gazpacho andaluz

One year I spent my post-Nutcracker lay-off in Seville, Spain and it was warm enough for restaurants to still have my favorite cold soup on the menu. I spent most lunches enjoying this classic spicy tomato-based soup in cafés along the large town square. It was particularly interesting because the week before New Year's Eve the square was filled with men sweeping cobblestones and the clamor of banging hammers as the stage was built for the New Year's celebration where people would toast in the new year with champagne and fruity sangria, feed each other fresh grapes for good luck, and dance the Sevillanes all night long.

I make variations of this soup often, adding some diced avocado or fresh crabmeat, or cold cooked lobster instead of croutons. Gazpacho made from juicy tomatoes is delicious any time of the year, but is especially refreshing when the weather is hot. This recipe can be made several hours ahead and chilled until serving.

Serves 4

2 slices day-old white or italian bread
3 large tomatoes, cored and diced
1 medium cucumber, peeled and cut in cubes
½ medium red onion, chopped
1 green or red bell pepper, seeded and chopped
2 tablespoons chopped fresh parsley
2 cloves garlic, crushed
2 cups tomato juice
3 tablespoons red wine vinegar
1 teaspoon paprika
½ teaspoon salt
freshly ground black pepper, to taste
2-3 drops hot red pepper sauce, optional

garlic croutons, for garnish
chopped fresh parsley, for garnish
finely chopped cucumber and red onion, for garnish

Only the pure of heart can make a good soup.
-Ludwig Van Beethoven

Soak bread in ½ cup water for 10 minutes. Place tomatoes, jalapeno, onion, cucumber, bell pepper, parsley, and garlic in the bowl of a food processor. Pulse several times to break up large chunks of vegetables. Add soaked bread, tomato juice, vinegar, paprika, and salt. Process 5 more seconds, or longer for a thinner soup. Add freshly ground pepper to taste and a drop at a time of red pepper sauce, until desired level of heat is reached. Stir well, then chill until ready to serve. (Or make by hand: Finely chop tomato, onion, cucumber, bell pepper, parsley, and garlic. Place in a large bowl and add soaked bread, tomato juice, vinegar, paprika, and salt. Stir well, then add freshly ground black pepper and one drop at a time of red pepper sauce to taste.) Chill soup thoroughly.
Serve soup in chilled bowls and top with croutons, chopped parsley, cucumber, and red onion.

gazpacho andaluz

sweet corn and coconut egg drop soup

This recipe was inspired by a lovely sweet corn and asparagus soup I often enjoyed at Mai's, a quiet little Vietnamese restaurant on Union Street in San Francisco. Unfortunately, the restaurant has since closed and like many of my recipes this one has been created out of necessity. The quite ordinary ingredients are transformed by a spoonful of nuoc mam, or Vietnamese fish sauce, and a swirl of coconut milk into a velvety soup, streaming with delicate threads of egg. It is fast and very easy to make and cooks in under 15 minutes. I can't live without it.

Serves 4

1 (14oz.) can cream-style corn
2 teaspoons vegetable oil
3 shallots, thinly sliced
2 scallions, thinly sliced
1 clove garlic, chopped
2 teaspoons nuoc mam (Vietnamese fish sauce)
½ cup whole corn kernels
salt to taste
2 cups lower-sodium non-fat chicken broth
1 cup water
1 tablespoon corn starch, dissolved into 1 tablespoon water
1 egg
3 tablespoons coconut milk
freshly ground black pepper

2 tablespoons fresh coriander leaves, stems removed, for garnish

Pour cream-style corn through a fine sieve to remove solids. Reserve purée.

Heat vegetable oil over medium-low heat in a large pot. Add shallots, scallions, and garlic and sauté until soft and aromatic, about 5 minutes. Add nuoc mam and sauté 1 minute.

Stir in reserved corn purée, whole corn, chicken broth, and 1 cup water. Season with salt and bring to a boil. Add cornstarch mixture and gently stir until soup thickens.

Crack egg into a small bowl and whisk with fork. Gently pour into boiling soup and stir for 1 minute. Add coconut milk and heat through. Season with freshly ground black pepper and ladle soup into bowls. Garnish with fresh coriander leaves.

saratoga sweet potato and ginger purée

One of my first auditions took place at the Saratoga Performing Arts Center in upstate New York. Two hundred little ten year olds with flowers in their hair who were as nervous as I was and a line of anxious mothers waiting outside the stage door to see which lucky six would get to perform Balanchine's famous ballet "Mozartiana" on the same stage as Suzanne Farrell. I carefully selected just the right leotard and spent an hour warming up in the hallway with a number pinned on my chest. When it was my turn, I was instructed to walk across the floor in front of the panel of judges and when I got to the other side, like 193 other hopefuls, I was simply told thank you very much. The day, however, was rewarding nonetheless, as I had a delicious and comforting lunch of sweet potato soup at a cozy restaurant called Mrs. London's. I have been making this rejuvenating soup ever since.

Serves 6-8

2 lbs. sweet potatoes, peeled and cut into large chunks
2 tablespoons sweet unsalted butter
2 medium onions, chopped
2 cups non-fat lower sodium chicken broth
1 teaspoon ground ginger
½ teaspoon salt
1 cup low-fat milk
freshly ground black pepper

Place potatoes in a large pot and cover with cold water. Bring to a boil, then lower heat and cook until potatoes are done, about 15 minutes. Drain potatoes and set aside. Rinse pot.
Melt butter in pot over low heat. Add onions and sauté until translucent. Add potatoes, chicken broth, ground ginger, and salt. Remove from heat.
Place cooled soup in the bowl of a food processor or blender, in batches if necessary. Pulse several times to break down mixture. Add milk, a half cup at a time, and process to a purée. Return soup to pot and season with freshly ground pepper. Reheat over low flame until heated through and serve.

portobello soup with rosemary

Serves 4

1 large onion, finely minced
2 lbs. white mushrooms, finely chopped
2 tablespoons butter
6 cups non-fat chicken broth
3 tablespoons arrowroot, dissolved in
2 tablespoons water
2 tablespoons fresh rosemary leaves, chopped
¼ cup minced fresh parsley
freshly ground black pepper
salt to taste

Sauté onion in butter over medium heat until soft. Add mushrooms and cook 3 minutes more, stirring occasionally. Add broth and simmer 10 minutes. Raise temperature just to a boil and stir in arrowroot mixture. Stir until soup thickens, about 2-3 minutes, then add rosemary and parsley. Season with salt and freshly ground pepper to taste. This soup often tastes better reheated the day after it is made.

portobello soup with rosemary

homemade chicken stock
for onion soup

1 whole chicken, 3 ½- 4 lbs., cut into pieces
2 tablespoons olive oil
½ cup white wine
4 quarts water
2 medium onions, sliced
2 stalks celery, sliced
2 medium carrots, peeled and sliced
1 leek, white part only, sliced
2 cloves garlic, smashed
2 teaspoons whole black peppercorns
3 sprigs parsley
3 sprigs fresh thyme
1 bay leaf
1 teaspoon salt

Heat olive oil in a large frying pan over medium-high heat. Brown chicken pieces on all sides, then transfer to a large stock pot. Add onions, celery, carrots, leek, and garlic and sauté until richly colored but not burned, about 5 minutes. Transfer vegetables to stock pot, then pour wine into frying pan. Cook wine for 1 minute, scraping up bits in the pan with a wooden spoon, then pour into stockpot with the chicken and vegetables. Pour water over to cover and add pepper-corns. Bring stock to a simmer. Skim any foam that rises to surface, then simmer 3 hours, skimming fat occasionally from the surface while cooking. After 3 hours add parsley, thyme, bay leaf, and salt and simmer another hour. Pour stock through a fine strainer and discard solids. Chill down quickly by placing pot into a bucket of ice or the refrigerator. Freeze extra stock in small containers to have on hand for adding to sauces and stir-fries.

udon with tiny gingered pork balls

Udon noodles and tiny ground pork balls perform the main role in this version of Japanese noodle soup, with enough crunchy crisp vegetables to round out the meal.

Serves 4

½ lb. lean ground pork or turkey
1 tablespoon minced fresh gingerroot
1 clove garlic, finely minced
1 teaspoon finely chopped jalapeno pepper
1 tablespoon low-sodium soy sauce
1 teaspoon toasted sesame seeds
8 oz. dried Japanese buckwheat soba or udon noodles
10 cups lower sodium chicken broth or home-made stock
2/3 cup drained canned straw mushrooms
2/3 cup drained and rinsed canned baby corn
2 cups raw broccoli florets
1 cup raw asparagus spears
½ cup raw trimmed snow or sugar snap peas
freshly ground black pepper

Combine ground meat, ginger, garlic, jalapeno, soy sauce, and sesame seeds in a medium bowl and mix well with hands. Form into small meatballs 1 inch in diameter. Set aside.
Bring chicken broth to a boil in a large pot and add pork balls. Turn heat to low and simmer 10 minutes. Add vegetables and simmer 3 minutes more. Season with freshly ground black pepper.
In another large pot, cook noodles according to package directions, then stir into soup. Serve immediately.

asian noodle soup with grilled chicken

I can't get enough of slurpy noodle soups served in big bowls. Canned vegetable or organic mushroom broth can be doctored into a fragrant soup base in a pinch by frying thinly sliced shallots and garlic in a wok, then combining with the broth. Add some cooked noodles, fresh vegetables and a few shrimp or sliced grilled chicken for quick but healthy fast food.

Serves 4

**2 boneless and skinless chicken breasts
salt and freshly ground black pepper
2 teaspoons vegetable oil
3 shallots, thinly sliced
1 teaspoon grated fresh ginger
½ small hot red chile pepper, seeded and chopped
2 cloves garlic, crushed
2 cups beef broth
4 cups vegetable or mushroom broth
½ cup fresh or drained canned oyster mushrooms, sliced
3 medium scallions, thinly sliced
1 cup fresh baby spinach leaves
10 oz. package ramen or chinese noodles, cooked according to package directions
2 tablespoons roasted sesame seeds**

Place chicken breasts between two large pieces of plastic and pound down with a meat tenderizer or rolling pin to ½ inch thickness. Season with salt and pepper and set aside.
Heat vegetable oil in a large soup pot. Sauté shallots, ginger, and chile pepper for about 2 minutes, until soft, then add garlic and mushrooms and cook 30 seconds more. Add beef and vegetable or mushroom broths and simmer 10 minutes over medium heat. While soup is simmering, grill or broil chicken for about 5 minutes on each side until cooked through. Transfer to a plate and cut into slices.
To serve: Divide spinach leaves among 4 large soup bowls. Add noodles and sliced scallions and ladle soup and sliced chicken across top and sprinkle with sesame seeds. Serve immediately.

chicken soup elixir

*As the curtain comes down on the last Nutcracker performance of the holiday season, it is time to relax and brew some soothing chicken soup. This is the soup that will cure what ails you, a remedy best made on the first day you've had off in weeks, when you can enjoy it's delicious smell throughout your home.
Homemade stock contains a fraction of the sodium of canned chicken broth and really isn't very troublesome to make. Make your stock into a meal by adding cooked chicken, a few diced carrots and leeks and cooked rice or noodles.*

Makes about 1 gallon

**1 tablespoon olive oil
1 whole chicken, 3 ½- 4 lbs., cleaned and excess fat removed
6 quarts cold water
2 medium carrots, scraped
1 large sweet vidalia onion, coarsely chopped
1 large yellow onion, chopped
2 stalks celery, trimmed
1 large leek, white part only, sliced
4 cloves garlic, peeled
6 juniper berries (optional)
2 teaspoons black peppercorns
1 large bunch parsley
3 sprigs fresh thyme or 1 teaspoon dried
2 bay leaves
1 teaspoon salt**

To make stock into soup add:
**2 carrots, scraped and sliced
½ cup small pasta, rice or egg noodles
8 oz. small button mushrooms
½ cup chopped fresh parsley**

Heat oil in a large stock pot. Add 2 scraped carrots, onions, celery, and leek and sauté until soft. Add chicken and cold water and bring to a boil. Make sure water is cold or stock will end up cloudy.
Turn heat to low and add remaining ingredients up to salt. Simmer 4-5 hours, stirring occasionally. Skim fat off the top, then strain soup through a fine sieve. Discard vegetables. For soup just add the remaining ingredients and simmer another 10 minutes.

asian noodle soup with grilled chicken

provençal potage of cannellini beans and potato

Serves 4-6

1 1/3 cups dried white cannellini beans
1 medium onion, peeled and cut in half
1 small bunch parsley
1 stalk celery, ends trimmed
2 carrots, scraped and trimmed
½ teaspoon salt
1 tablespoon walnut or vegetable oil
1 medium onion, peeled and sliced
½ cup sliced leek, white part only
2 large potatoes, peeled and cut into chunks
4 cups chicken stock or lower-sodium canned broth
1 sprig fresh thyme
1 bay leaf
1 small bunch parsley
2 cloves garlic, crushed
1 dried red pepper
salt and freshly ground white pepper
½ cup low-fat milk
pinch ground nutmeg
¼ cup chopped fresh parsley

The night before: Rinse and pick through beans to remove any debris. Place beans in a medium size bowl and cover with warm water. Let stand at room temperature overnight.

The next day: Drain beans and place in a large pot with halved onion, parsley, celery stalk, whole carrot, and ½ teaspoon salt. Cover with 4 cups water and bring to a boil. Reduce heat to medium-low, cover and cook 30 minutes or until tender. Remove from heat. Discard cooked celery, onion, and parsley. Cut carrots into slices and set aside. Drain beans, reserving 3 cups cooking liquid.

Make a bouquet garnis by tying the thyme, bay leaf, and parsley together with string.

Heat oil in a large pot. Add sliced onion and leek and sauté just until soft but not brown. Add beans, reserved cooking liquid, potatoes, chicken stock, bouquet garnis, garlic, and red pepper. Bring to a boil, then reduce heat to medium and cook until potatoes are tender, about 15 minutes. Discard bouquet garnis and red pepper. Let soup cool, then place half in a food processor or blender and pulse just to break up large pieces, or more if you like a thinner texture.

Return soup to pot. Add carrots, milk, and ¼ cup chopped fresh parsley. Heat through. Season with salt and freshly ground white pepper. Ladle into soup bowls and garnish with a pinch of freshly grated nutmeg.

curried pumpkin soup

Pumpkin is a quite versatile root vegetable rich in Vitamin A. This satisfying low-fat soup will fool even the richest tastebuds.

Serves 8

1 tablespoon sweet unsalted butter
2 small onions, chopped
2 cloves garlic, finely minced
½ - ¾ teaspoon curry powder, to taste
½ teaspoon salt
¼ teaspoon ground white pepper
2 ¾ cups non-fat lower sodium chicken broth
1 (15oz.) can pumpkin
1 cup skimmed evaporated milk (regular low-fat milk can be substituted)

Melt butter in a large heavy pot over medium-low heat. Add chopped onions and sauté until golden, stirring often so they don't stick to the bottom of the pot. Add garlic and sauté 1 minute more, then add curry powder, salt, and white pepper. Cook, stirring, for 1 minute.
Add pumpkin and chicken broth. Cool soup, then transfer in batches to a blender or food processor and purée just until smooth. Return to pot. Simmer 10 minutes. Add evaporated milk and warm over low heat until heated through. Serve with crusty bread.

easy split pea soup

Split pea is one of the easiest soups to make, just throw the ingredients in a pot and simmer until done. As this soup tends to thicken with refrigeration, add a little water when reheating.

Serves 8

1 lb. dried green split peas, rinsed in a colander
2 quarts non-fat low-sodium chicken or vegetable broth
1 quart water
2 medium red or yellow onions, chopped
3 large cloves garlic, crushed
¾ teaspoon italian seasoning or dried oregano leaves
¼ - ½ teaspoon white pepper
1/8 teaspoon freshly ground black pepper
2 bay leaves
2 cups sliced carrots, optional

In a large pot, combine everything except carrots. Simmer uncovered 75 minutes, skimming surface occasionally.
Add carrots if using and simmer another 15 minutes. Season with salt and freshly ground black pepper and serve.

fouetté

Third
Salads: (Not just rabbit food!)

It is a fallacy to say dancers eat nothing but carrots and lettuce. In truth, we love food and crave masses of it -- we just don't want it to show when we have to put on a leotard. Demanding roles require a lot of energy, and while a ten minute jog may not seem all that strenuous, the precision and concentration required to perform a ten minute solo can feel like running a marathon! Salads are the perfect energy food, with endless possibilities of combinations. Anything green is a blank canvas, from irony spinach to peppery rocket, prim slim green beans or frilly frissé, the lettuce leaf is a base on which to build a plate of vibrant tastes and textures, and vegetables are only the beginning. From curried chicken with chunks of apple and tart dried cranberries to lean succulent breast of duck, the following salads are a feast to the eyes as well as the stomach. Salads are the great compromise for large appetites, healthy and generous servings packed with the nutrition required for peak performance.

grilled tuna, crab and potato salad with fresh dill vinaigrette
vietnamese chicken salad
grilled chicken salad with spicy blackberry dressing
taboulleh with shredded baby spinach
panzanella
spicy broccoli
bravo salad
hearts of romaine with sesame ginger dressing
spinach salad with feta, almonds and black mission fig vinaigrette
salmagundi
thai eggplant salad with pickled garlic
curried chicken salad with apples, dried cranberries and toasted walnuts
asian red cabbage slaw
duck breast salad with orange oil
thai carrot salad
spring salad
gado gado

grilled tuna, crab and potato salad with fresh dill vinaigrette

A special appetizer I ate in a little Greenwich Village restaurant inspired this sophisticated salad. I replaced the olive oil and mustard vinaigrette with a fresh dill and yoghurt dressing, for a fresh bite with less fat. The key to this salad is the freshness of the ingredients-- be sure to use sashimi-grade tuna. The potatoes and tuna can be made ahead of time and assembled with the other ingredients just before serving.

Serves 4

12 oz. fresh tuna steak
2 teaspoons olive oil
freshly ground black pepper
8 oz. fresh or canned white crabmeat, flaked
2 medium cooked yukon gold or red new potatoes, cut into small cubes
½ fresh red bell pepper, finely chopped
2 tablespoons chopped fresh dill
1 small stalk fresh endive
8 cups fresh mixed organic greens (mesclun or mixed red leaf lettuce, radiccio, and arugula)

dressing:
1/3 cup fresh dill, stems removed
1 ½ tablespoons white wine vinegar
1 ½ teaspoons olive oil
2/3 cup non-fat plain yoghurt
1 teaspoon dijon mustard
2 cloves garlic, minced
salt and freshly ground black pepper to taste

fresh dill sprigs for garnish

Rub both sides of tuna steak with 1 teaspoon olive oil and sprinkle with freshly ground black pepper.
Heat remaining teaspoon olive oil in a small skillet over high heat. Sear tuna 1 minute on each side then transfer to a plate. Cut into thin slices.
Whisk together all dressing ingredients in a small bowl or process in a small food processor until smooth, about 5 seconds.
Divide salad ingredients among 4 plates. Drizzle dressing on top.

grilled tuna, crab and potato salad
with fresh dill vinaigrette

vietnamese chicken salad

The Vietnamese food craze had not yet hit Manhattan before I moved to San Francisco from New York City and this exciting cuisine was one of my favorite gastronomic discoveries. There was nothing more refreshing after a long day of dancing than relaxing in a cool restaurant amid the intoxicating perfume of chiles, jasmine rice, and fresh herbs. One of my favorite dishes was chicken salad, with a dressing both sweet and sharp that beautifully sets off the varied tastes and textures of vegetables, noodles, and finely shredded chicken.

Serves 4

1 large boneless, skinless chicken breast
2 cups non-fat chicken broth
½ medium head green cabbage, finely shredded
4 scallions, thinly sliced
½ cup cilantro leaves
4 oz. thin rice vermicelli or cellophane (bean thread) noodles
6 cloves garlic, sliced paper thin
2 shallots, thinly sliced
1 tablespoon peanut oil
¼ cup unsalted peanuts, chopped

dressing:
4 tablespoons seasoned rice vinegar
juice of 2 limes
4 tablespoons pink grapefruit juice
2 teaspoons sugar
2 tablespoons fresh cilantro leaves, finely chopped
freshly ground black pepper

Bring chicken broth to a simmer in a shallow saucepan. Add chicken and reduce heat to very low. Simmer until cooked, 8-10 minutes. Transfer to a plate and let cool to room temperature, then shred with fingers and set aside. Discard broth.

Soak rice noodles in boiling water until soft, about 10 minutes. Drain well and set aside.

Whisk dressing ingredients in a small bowl until sugar is dissolved.

Heat peanut oil in a medium sauté pan over medium heat. Add shallots and sauté over medium-low heat until nicely browned, about 4 minutes, then add garlic and cook until caramelized, another minute or two.

Toss cabbage, chicken, noodles, cilantro, scallions, and enough dressing to coat salad. Mix in shallots and garlic. Just before serving, season with lots of freshly ground pepper and top with chopped peanuts.

vietnamese chicken salad

grilled chicken salad with spicy blackberry dressing

When my friend Tulsa Ballet Theatre principal dancer Melanie Nasser severely injured her knee landing from a jump in class one day, she ended up spending the season exercising her culinary skills instead of dancing. My favorite recipe was her simple green salad mixed with blackberries and sweet yellow peppers.

In this recipe I use seedless blackberry fruit spread and jalapeno peppers as the base for a sweet spicy dressing that is great for hot weather, served over grilled breast of chicken on a bed of peppery arugula, sweet yellow bell peppers, and sliced mushrooms. Toasted pine nuts add crunch.

This recipe also works well with seedless raspberry fruit spread.

Serves 4

1 large whole boneless, skinless breast of chicken
salt and freshly ground black pepper
1 teaspoon vegetable oil
10 oz. fresh arugula leaves, washed and dried
1 fresh yellow bell pepper, cored, seeded and sliced
8 fresh mushrooms, thinly sliced
½ cup toasted pine nuts

blackberry dressing:(Makes about 1 1/3 cups)

2 cloves garlic, minced
½ small jalapeno pepper, seeded and minced
2/3 cup seedless blackberry jam or fruit spread
4 tablespoons balsamic vinegar
2 teaspoons vegetable oil
2 tablespoons freshly squeezed lime juice
4 tablespoons water

Make dressing: Place garlic and jalapeno in a small food processor and pulse to chop. Add remaining dressing ingredients and process until smooth. Set aside until ready to use.

Season chicken with salt and pepper. Rub with oil and grill or broil chicken until cooked through, about 8-10 minutes per side. Cut into slices and keep warm.

Toss together arugula, pepper, mushrooms, and pine nuts in a large bowl with enough dressing to coat. Arrange salad on plates and top with sliced chicken. Drizzle a little more dressing over top and serve.

grilled chicken salad with spicy blackberry dressing

taboulleh with shredded baby spinach

Most deli versions of this middle eastern grain salad are deceptively loaded with olive oil and contain far more fat and calories than you would expect. This sneaky recipe replaces much of the oil with nonfat yoghurt and is enriched with baby spinach for an added boost of iron. Taboulleh cooks easily and makes great picnic food.

Serves 4

1 cup (6oz.) bulgar wheat
1 teaspoon salt
1 ¼ cups boiling water
3 tablespoons freshly squeezed lemon juice
2 tablespoons olive oil
3 tablespoons plain nonfat yoghurt
2 cloves finely minced garlic
freshly ground pepper
1 cup chopped seeded tomatoes
1 cup diced english cucumber
½ cup thinly sliced green onions
½ cup chopped flat-leaf italian parsley
¼ cup chopped fresh mint leaves
½ cup raw baby spinach, cut into very-thin strips
salt to taste
8 leaves romaine lettuce

Place bulgar and salt in a medium bowl and pour in boiling water. Cover tightly and let stand 30 minutes.
In another small bowl, whisk together lemon juice, olive oil, and yoghurt. Add garlic and freshly ground pepper to taste and whisk again. Add to cooked bulgar and mix well. Season with salt and freshly ground pepper. Cover and chill 2 hours.
Just before serving: Toss bulgar together with tomatoes, cucumber, onions, parsley, mint, and spinach. Serve chilled or at room temperature, spooned onto lettuce leaves.

panzanella

I use leftover bread to make this summer-fresh Italian salad. The ingredients can be varied to include other fresh herbs such as marjoram or oregano instead of the basil, or grilling the peppers before adding makes a nice antipasto. To make this salad more substantial, add some cubes of italian fontina or diced Italian salami.

Serves 6

½ loaf day-old italian or french bread, toasted and cut into cubes
3 ripe tomatoes, diced
1 yellow tomato, diced
½ medium cucumber, peeled and cubed
1 small green bell pepper, seeded and diced
1 small yellow or orange bell pepper, seeded and diced
¼ cup red or vidalia onion, sliced

dressing:
¼ cup red wine vinegar
1 teaspoon lemon juice
2 tablespoons fresh basil, shredded
3 cloves garlic, crushed
salt and freshly ground black pepper to taste
¼ cup extra-virgin olive oil

Make dressing by whisking together vinegar, lemon juice, basil, garlic and olive oil.
In a large bowl, toss remaining ingredients. Add dressing and mix well. Divide among plates and serve.

panzanella

O body swayed to music, O brightening glance,
How can we know the dancer from the dance?
-William Butler Yeats

spicy broccoli

This sesame and soy marinade spices up lightly steamed broccoli for a great side salad for picnics. Broccoli is high in calcium, which is always good for dancers to help prevent stress fractures. Steam the florets just until they are bright green so they stay crunchy and retain their nutrients.

Serves 4-6

2 large bunches broccoli florets
½ large hot red chile pepper, seeded and slivered
½ cup sliced green onions
3 tablespoons low sodium soy sauce
1 tablespoon rice vinegar
2 tablespoons toasted sesame oil
1 tablespoon spicy sesame oil or red chili oil
¼ teaspoon chili garlic sauce
2 teaspoons toasted sesame seeds
2 teaspoons black sesame seeds

Steam broccoli over rapidly boiling water 3 minutes, until crisp and bright green. Drain and rinse with cold water.
Toss broccoli with red pepper and green onions and set aside. Stir together soy sauce, vinegar, oils, and chili garlic sauce. Toss with broccoli and sesame seeds. Let stand 15 minutes before serving.

bravo salad

I used to enjoy gala performances because there was always a party after the show. It was interesting to meet people in the audience, especially because they rarely recognized the performers offstage. It was always fascinating to me as a dancer to both physically and emotionally expose myself onstage and somehow remain relatively anonymous once the curtain was down.
This salad was served at a fund-raising gala for Ohio Ballet.

Serves 4-6

1 medium head butter lettuce
1/3 cup mixed dried strawberries, cranberries, blueberries, cherries and raisins
1 medium tomato, sliced
¼ cup halved toasted walnuts
1 small endive
2 oz. hearts of palm, cubed

raspberry walnut dressing:
¼ cup raspberry vinegar
2 tablespoons walnut oil
1 teaspoon dijon mustard
3 tablespoons orange juice
½ teaspoon honey
1 clove garlic, crushed
salt and freshly ground white pepper

Whisk dressing ingredients together well with a fork. Season with salt and pepper.
Divide salad ingredients among plates. Drizzle with dressing and serve.

hearts of romaine with sesame ginger dressing

Several dancers and I used to get together when one of us was retiring or joining another ballet company for a farewell dinner, usually at a Japanese restaurant. This recipe was inspired by a wonderful ginger house dressing I used to order, though since I created this version at home my friends come to my house instead and keep asking when I am going to bottle it. It happens to also be low in fat and is delicious as well as a marinade for chicken.

Serves 4

8 cups sliced hearts of romaine lettuce
1 large carrot, shredded
½ cup red cabbage, finely shredded
1 medium tomato, sliced

dressing:
5 oz. sesame salad dressing, (preferably Mitsukan brand Wafu dressing Goma)
2 inches fresh ginger, peeled
2 tablespoons rice wine
2 tablespoons rice vinegar
2-3 tablespoons fat-free bottled thousand island dressing
1 tablespoon orange juice
1 teaspoon grated orange zest

Place all dressing ingredients in a blender and process until smooth. Divide vegetables among plates and drizzle with dressing.

spinach salad with feta, almonds and black mission fig vinaigrette

Really fresh dried black mission figs will make a smoother dressing. Soak them in boiling water for 5 minutes or so until they plump up, then liquefy in a blender before adding remaining dressing ingredients.

Serves 4
**3 tablespoons flaked almonds
1 teaspoon butter
10 oz. fresh baby spinach leaves
2 tablespoons dried cranberries
1/3 cup reduced fat or regular feta cheese, crumbled**

**fig vinaigrette:
¼ cup dried black mission figs
¼ cup balsamic vinegar
½ cup extra-virgin olive oil
1 teaspoon honey
salt and freshly ground white pepper to taste**

Soak figs in ½ cup boiling water for 5 minutes then place figs and soaking juice in a blender and process to a purée. Add remaining dressing ingredients and blend until liquefied. (Add a little water if dressing seems too thick.) Set aside.
Heat butter in a small skillet. Add almonds and saute just until lightly toasted. Transfer to a large bowl to cool, then mix with spinach, cranberries, and feta. Toss with just enough dressing to coat leaves and serve at once.

salmagundi

The name of this salad comes from the French word salmagondis, meaning potpourri, and can contain any assortment of chopped cooked meats, eggs, pickles, and fresh vegetables. Lemony caper vinaigrette finishes this ancient salade composé, or arranged salad, which is perfect for al fresco lunches and picnics.

Serves 4

salad:
**½ cup gerkins or cornichons
8 quail eggs, hard-boiled or 2 regular hard-boiled chicken eggs, sliced
¼ cup pickled pearl onions
½ cup green beans
½ granny smith apple, sliced
¼ cup red or green grapes, sliced in half
½ red bell pepper, sliced
1 small head butter lettuce
3 radiccio leaves
2 cups cold cooked chicken or turkey breast
½ cup lean cubed ham
¼ cup green olives, optional**

lemon-caper vinaigrette:
**3 tablespoons cup freshly squeezed lemon juice
½ cup extra-virgin olive oil
1 tablespoon tiny capers, drained
salt and freshly ground black pepper to taste**

snipped fresh chives, for garnish

Whisk together all dressing ingredients and set aside. Blanch green beans for one minute in salted boiling water and drain. Let cool.
Place butter lettuce and radiccio on plates or a large platter. Arrange remaining salad ingredients over lettuces. Drizzle with dressing to taste and serve immediately.

duck breast salad with sesame orange oil

I used to think duck was strictly off-limits due to its thick layer of fat. One nice thing about training to cook fine French cuisine is that deep within those butter and cream laden masterpieces, I find great potential for recipes I can actually eat and enjoy without visions of tightening jeans haunting me. Needless to say, I have turned enthusiastic convert when it comes to duck breast. With the skin removed, the meat is luxurious and rich without the heaviness you get from eating beef or the blandness that can often happen with pork or turkey. A light drizzle of orange and a spark of five-spice is all it takes for this salad to taste exquisite and still be deceptively light.

Serves 4

2 duck breasts
salt and freshly ground black pepper
2 teaspoons finely grated orange zest
3 tablespoons extra-virgin olive oil
½ teaspoon finely grated fresh gingeroot
1 hot dried red chile
½ teaspoon chinese five-spice powder
½ teaspoon light brown sugar
juice of one orange
segments from 1 large orange, skin removed
1 teaspoon toasted sesame oil
4 cups mixed greens (baby spinach, arugula, watercress, lambs lettuce)

Rub orange zest onto both sides of duck breasts. Season with salt and freshly ground black pepper, then pan fry in 1 tablespoon olive oil until medium-rare, about 4 minutes on each side. Transfer to a dish and keep warm. Heat remaining 2 tablespoons olive oil in a small pan. When hot add dried chile. Add five-spice and cook another 2-3 seconds, then add ginger and brown sugar. Stir once then remove from heat and let cool. Discard chile and whisk in orange juice and sesame oil.
Toss dressing with mixed greens and orange segments and arrange on plates. Thinly slice duck and place over greens to serve.

Cooking is not simply in the tongue,
in the palate
it is in the whole body
flowing out of the groin and chest
through arms and hands

-Edward Espe Brown

duck breast salad with sesame orange oil

thai carrot salad

One of the most enjoyable aspects of dancing in New York City was the diversity of cultures and cuisines to which I was exposed. Dancers came from all over the world and their culinary influences were often displayed by the contents of their lunchboxes. This salad was one of my favorites: varied textures of crunchy vegetables in an oil-free Thai lime dressing. The recipe comes from a fellow dancer from Singapore.

Serves 4-6

1 ½ lbs. carrots, peeled and shredded
8 oz. string beans, trimmed and cut into 1 inch pieces
1 medium ripe tomato, sliced
1 clove garlic, crushed and thinly sliced
½-1 small jalapeno pepper, seeded and finely minced
juice of 2 limes
1 tablespoon fish sauce (nam pla)
½ teaspoon palm or light brown sugar
½ cup unsalted peanuts, chopped

Combine carrots, string beans, and sliced tomato in a large bowl. Add minced garlic and toss to combine.
In a small bowl whisk together minced jalapeno, lime juice, fish sauce, and sugar until sugar is dissolved. Toss with carrot mixture and let stand 15 minutes to develop flavor.
Sprinkle chopped peanuts on top of salad just before serving.

spring salad

I adore those delicious rice paper rolls in Vietnamese restaurants, artful parcels of crunchy bean sprouts, fragrant fresh herbs, plump shrimp and thin rice noodles, but when I don't feel like taking the time to soak each rice paper wrapper I make this salad, spiked with a chile pepper and lime dressing.

Serves 4

6 oz. dried rice sticks, buckwheat somen noodles, linguini, or other asian noodles
8 large cooked shrimp, cleaned and shelled with tails left on
4 oz. high-quality cooked crab meat
½ raw turnip, peeled and shredded
1 carrot, peeled and shredded
2 green onions, thinly sliced
1 cup fresh bean sprouts
½ cup fresh mint leaves
1/3 cup fresh coriander leaves
1 small head butter lettuce or 4 large leaves red or green leaf lettuce
3 tablespoons roasted unsalted peanuts, coarsely chopped

2 egg pancakes (recipe follows)

dressing:
½ fresh red or green chile pepper, trimmed, seeded and coarsely chopped
1 ½ tablespoons sugar
¼ cup rice vinegar
¼ cup nuoc mam (Asian fish sauce)
2 cloves garlic, crushed
1 tablespoon freshly squeezed lime juice
freshly ground black pepper

egg pancakes:
2 eggs
¼ teaspoon nuoc mam
½ teaspoon water
freshly ground black pepper

Make dressing by whisking or processing in a blender all dressing ingredients until sugar is dissolved and garlic and chile are finely minced. Set aside.

For the egg pancakes place eggs, nuoc mam, water, and pepper in a bowl. Whisk well with a fork. Spray a crêpe pan or small skillet with vegetable oil cooking spray and heat over medium-high heat. When pan is hot pour in half the egg mixture and immediately tilt pan back and forth to coat bottom. Cook about 20 seconds, or until edges begin to look dry, then quickly flip to other side with a spatula. Cook another 20 seconds, or until light golden and cooked through. Transfer to a cutting board and repeat with remaining egg mixture. Roll cooked pancakes into a cylinder and cut crosswise into thin strips. Set aside.

Bring a large pot of water to a boil. Add noodles and bring water back to the boil. Cook noodles until soft, about 3 minutes, then drain a colander and refresh with cold water. If you are using a different noodles other than rice sticks, cook them according to package directions, then drain and set aside until ready to use. (Stir in a teaspoon of vegetable oil into noodles if not using right away to prevent them from sticking together.)

In a large bowl, combine noodles, shrimp, crabmeat, turnip, carrots, green onions, bean sprouts, mint, and coriander leaves. Add just enough dressing to coat and toss gently.

Divide lettuce among plates and top with shrimp and noodle mixture. Garnish with egg pancake strips and chopped peanuts and serve immediately.

spring salad

gado gado

(indonesian vegetable salad with warm peanut sauce)

The traditional version of this colorful Indonesian salad calls for deep-fried tofu and a warm peanut dressing made with cream of coconut, garlic, and brown sugar. I pan-fry the tofu just until crispy and for the dressing use a combination of light coconut milk and fat-free evaporated skimmed milk, which reduces the fat content without losing any of its rich taste.

This salad is a great way to serve a variety of vegetables for a healthy summer lunch or first course for dinner. Preparation time can be shortened greatly by making the components in advance. The dressing will keep several days in the refrigerator and the eggs and potatoes can be boiled several hours before serving. Reheat dressing a minute or two in the microwave or in a small pot for about 5 minutes over low heat.

Serves 4-6

1 lb. firm tofu
2 large idaho potatoes or 4-5 small red new potatoes
1 cup sliced or shredded peeled carrots
1 cup raw string beans, trimmed
1 cup raw asparagus spears, trimmed
2 cups red or green cabbage, shredded
1 large ripe tomato, sliced or ½ cup cherry or grape tomatoes
½ medium cucumber, thinly sliced
3 hard-cooked eggs, sliced
vegetable oil cooking spray

warm peanut dressing: Makes about 1 1/3 cups

1 clove garlic, minced
½ fresh hot green chile, seeded and minced
1 teaspoon fresh gingeroot, minced
¼ teaspoon paprika
1/8 teaspoon ground turmeric
dash cayenne pepper
¼ teaspoon salt
1 teaspoon vegetable oil
½ cup light or regular coconut milk
½ cup fat-free evaporated skimmed milk
½ teaspoon brown or palm sugar
¼ cup creamy reduced-fat peanut butter
1 teaspoon low-sodium soy sauce
1 tablespoon freshly squeezed lime juice
1-2 tablespoons water

Prepare dressing: In the bowl of a small food processor or with a mortar and pestle, make a paste from the garlic, chile, gingeroot, paprika, turmeric, cayenne, and salt. Heat oil in a saucepan. Add spice paste and cook 1 minute, stirring to prevent burning. Add coconut milk, evaporated milk, and brown or palm sugar.
Turn heat to very low and simmer 5 minutes, until slightly thickened. (Do not boil.) Remove from heat and whisk in peanut butter, soy sauce, and lime juice until smooth. Let stand at room temperature 15 minutes. Stir in a tablespoon or two of water if dressing is too thick.

To make the salad first remove excess moisture from tofu by wrapping with several sheets of paper towels. Place wrapped block on a plate and weigh down with a large can balanced on another plate so weight is evenly distributed over tofu. Let sit at least 1 hour. Drain off liquid and discard paper towels. Cut tofu into cubes and set aside.

Scrub potatoes and cut into chunks (or leave whole for small potatoes). Place in a medium pot and cover with water. Bring to a rapid boil then lower heat and cook until done, about 15 minutes. Drain and set aside.

Bring a large pot of salted water to a rapid boil. Line up carrots, string beans, asparagus, and cabbage. When water reaches a boil, add carrots and cook 1 minute, then add string beans and asparagus and cook two more minutes. Remove vegetables with a slotted spoon and run cold water over them to stop cooking process. Bring pot of water back to a boil and add cabbage. Blanch 1 minute and drain into colander. Refresh cabbage with cold water and set aside.

Spray a small pan with vegetable oil spray and heat over medium-low heat. Add cubed tofu and cook until golden on all sides.

Thinly slice cooked and cooled potatoes. To serve, reheat dressing gently over very low heat in a saucepan or in the microwave for 1-2 minutes. Arrange sliced potatoes, blanched vegetables, tomato, and cucumber decoratively or layer in a ring mold onto 4-6 large plates. Scatter fried tofu on the side. Chop or press hard-boiled egg through a sieve and sprinkle over tops of salads. Serve immediately with warm peanut dressing.

développé

Fourth

There's No Meat on Us!

Vegetarian and Meatless Dishes

Today even the most classical ballet companies perform modern and contemporary works and as a dancer, one must be versatile and able to adapt to different styles of movement, just as to eat a healthy diet, one must have a proper balance of a wide variety of foods. Dancers follow many types of diets, from macrobiotic and vegetarian to high-protein and high-carbohydrate, depending on their body-type and the stamina required for particular roles. Throughout my career I have been privy to many diets that work, and those that don't, and since I hate to diet I love recipes that are big on flavor without making me gain weight. These meatless dishes will satisfy both vegetarians and the most strict meat and potato eaters, and whether you must dance to live or live to eat, these recipes will surely keep you on your toes!

fresh spinach, roasted eggplant, and mushroom lasagna
miso sesame noodles
rigatoni with zucchini and uncooked tomato sauce
farfalle with shiitake mushroom and herb cream sauce
pizza marguerita with capers and red onion
curried banana balls with masoor daal
crêpes ratatouille
southwestern black bean and polenta burritos with fresh tomato salsa
georgia sweetcorn pudding
italian fontina, parmesan, and potato gratin
cold sesame soba with tofu
thai coconut rice
sweet potato mash with green chile and brown mustard seeds
grilled zucchini with garlic and fresh thyme
garlic mushrooms

fresh spinach, roasted eggplant, and mushroom lasagna

This outstanding vegetarian lasagna is perfect for entertaining and is so delicious you will never crave fatty meat versions again. I usually simplify preparation by making the marinara and white sauces ahead of time so I can assemble it quickly on the day I plan to serve it. It can also be made up to the point of baking and frozen for up to two weeks.

Serves 8

lasagna:
1 large eggplant, sliced into ¼ inch strips
2 medium onions
2 teaspoons extra-virgin olive oil
1(12oz.) box fresh mushrooms, cleaned and sliced
1 teaspoon dried oregano leaves
20 oz. fresh spinach, washed with trimmed or 2 (10½ oz.) packages frozen chopped spinach
4 fresh thyme sprigs (or ½ teaspoon dried)
¼ cup white wine
¼ cup fresh basil leaves, ripped into small pieces
2 cloves garlic, finely minced
salt & freshly ground pepper
1/3 cup + ¼ cup fresh parsley, chopped
½ pound lasagne noodles
¾ pound (12oz.) part-skim mozzarella, shredded
½ cup (2 oz.) fresh parmesan cheese, grated
1 recipe marinara sauce
1 recipe white sauce
olive oil cooking spray or olive oil

marinara sauce:
2 small onions, minced
3 garlic cloves, finely chopped
3 tablespoons extra-virgin olive oil
2 (28oz.) cans whole peeled Italian tomatoes
¼ teaspoon sugar
¼ teaspoon salt
freshly ground pepper

In a large saucepan, cook onions and garlic in olive oil over medium heat until soft and golden, about 5 minutes. Drain liquid from cans of tomatoes and squeeze each tomato gently to remove seeds. Chop coarsely and stir into the onion and garlic mixture, along with sugar, salt, and freshly ground pepper to taste. Simmer covered, over low heat for 25 minutes, stirring occasionally. Set aside.

white sauce:
2 ½ cups low-fat milk
3 tablespoons unsalted butter
4 tablespoons flour
¼ teaspoon salt
freshly ground pepper
freshly ground nutmeg

Scald milk over medium-high heat. Cover and set aside. In another saucepan, melt butter over low heat. Add flour, a tablespoon at a time, whisking after each addition. Continue whisking for 2 minutes. Add hot milk, whisking constantly. Simmer 5 minutes over medium-low heat, stirring occasionally as sauce thickens. Add salt, pepper, and nutmeg to taste. Remove from heat. Transfer to a small bowl and cover with plastic wrap if not using immediately. Makes enough for one recipe lasagne.

fresh spinach, roasted eggplant
and mushroom lasagna

To assemble lasagna:

Preheat broiler. Place eggplant strips close together on broiling tray (do in two batches if necessary). Spray with cooking spray or brush lightly with olive oil and sprinkle with salt. Place under broiler for 10 minutes, or until strips are nicely charred, but not burned. Turn strips over with spatula and repeat. Set aside. In a large skillet, cook onions in 1 tablespoon olive oil until soft and golden, 5 minutes or so. Add mushrooms, white wine, oregano, leaves from fresh thyme sprigs, fresh minced basil, salt and freshly ground pepper to taste. (Hold one end of thyme sprig with two fingers and gently squeeze down the stem to remove leaves.) Cook stirring, until liquid evaporates. Add garlic and spinach and cook for 3-5 minutes more. If all spinach doesn't fit into pan at once, add half at a time, sauté with mushrooms until wilted, then add remaining half, stirring quickly to incorporate. Mix well with one recipe White Sauce and 1/3 cup parsley and set aside.

Meanwhile, cook lasagne according to directions on package until it is al dente. Rinse in cool water and keep slightly wet to keep from sticking.

Preheat oven to 400 degrees. In a rectangular casserole dish (13x10x2 inches), spread 1cup marinara sauce evenly over bottom. Cover with a single layer of lasagne noodles (shake off excess water before putting noodles into dish), then spread half of the spinach-mushroom mixture.

Top with a layer of half the roasted eggplant, then sprinkle with half the mozzarella and half the parmesan cheese. Repeat as above, starting with another layer of noodles, followed by the remaining spinach-mushroom mixture. Top with remaining eggplant, and half of the remaining mozzarella and parmesan cheeses. Add remaining noodles, then spread remaining marinara sauce evenly over top. Sprinkle the rest of the mozzarella and parmesan and cover with tin foil.

Bake 35 minutes or until sauce bubbles at the edges. Let rest 10 minutes before serving. Garnish with remaining ¼ cup chopped parsley.

miso sesame noodles

These tangy noodles are dressed with a base of white miso instead of the usual lathering of high fat sesame paste, which gives a unique rich taste and a fraction of the fat of recipes in Chinese restaurants.

Serves 4

1 (10 oz.) package chinese noodles or linguini
½ red bell pepper, seeded and finely minced
2 large scallions, thinly sliced
½ medium cucumber, peeled, seeded and shredded

sesame sauce:
½ inch piece fresh ginger, peeled
1 large clove fresh garlic, peeled
1 large scallion, trimmed
3 tablespoons white miso
1 ½ tablespoons honey
2 teaspoons dijon mustard
3 tablespoons chicken broth or vegetable stock
1 tablespoon lower sodium soy sauce
½ teaspoon sesame oil

Combine fresh ginger, garlic, and one large scallion in the bowl of a small food processor and pulse several times until well chopped. Add remaining sauce ingredients and purée until fairly smooth, about 15 seconds. Set aside.

Cook noodles according to package directions. Drain and rinse with cool water. Toss noodles with shredded bell pepper, sliced scallions and shredded cucumber. Pour dressing over noodles and mix well. Let stand 30 minutes before serving.

miso sesame noodles

rigatoni with with zucchini and uncooked tomato sauce

Serves 4

1 (28oz.) can Italian whole plum tomatoes
2 tablespoons plus 2 teaspoons olive oil
2 tablespoons chopped fresh parsley
1 tablespoon chopped fresh basil
½ teaspoon salt
1 large clove fresh garlic, finely minced
freshly ground pepper
1 lb. pasta (rigatoni, rotelli, or ziti)
2 small or 1 large zucchini, shredded
6 oz. part-skim mozzarella, cut into small cubes
¼ cup walnuts
2 tablespoons chopped fresh parsley

Cut tomatoes in half and squeeze gently to remove seeds. Chop coarsely and place in a bowl with 2 tablespoons olive oil, parsley, basil, salt, garlic, and freshly ground pepper to taste. Let stand at room temperature for 1 hour. In a small skillet, toast walnuts over low heat until a few shades darker, then chop coarsely and set aside. Sauté zucchini in 2 teaspoons olive oil in a saucepan over medium-high heat for 1 minute, then remove from heat and stir into tomato sauce. Bring a large pot of water to a rapid boil and cook pasta according to package directions. Drain hot cooked pasta and toss with cubed tomato sauce and mozzarella. Divide among plates and serve sprinkled with toasted walnuts and parsley.

Note: This pasta can be served warm, at room temperature or cold, but be sure to add the walnuts just before eating so they stay crunchy.

farfalle with shiitake mushroom and herb cream sauce

For a quick and casual supper buy some festive looking gourmet pasta and sauté this quick cream sauce in a wok. It takes about the same time to make as it takes the pasta to cook, so its a great dish when you don't want to spend much time in the kitchen. Serve with a leafy green salad and a crisp chianti.

Serves 4

½ oz. fresh shiitake mushrooms, sliced thinly
8 oz. fresh button mushrooms, cleaned and sliced
2 tablespoons extra-virgin olive oil
2 cloves garlic, minced
2 tablespoons minced fresh herbs, chopped
(I use a combination of oregano and thyme leaves)
½ cup dry white wine
1 ½ cups chicken broth
½ cup heavy cream
salt & freshly ground black or white pepper

1 lb. fresh hot cooked farfalle or other pasta

Heat oil in a wok over high heat. Add mushrooms and let them sear for 2 minutes without stirring. Add garlic and wine and sauté quickly until wine is reduced by half. Add stock and cream and let simmer another 2 minutes. Stir in fresh herbs and season with salt and pepper. Toss with hot cooked pasta and serve at once.

pizza marguerita with capers and red onion

When I was given the opportunity to perform Balanchine's Tchaikovsky Pas de Deux in Spoleto, Italy, I couldn't wait to dance in the romantic Theatro Nuovo. The theatre was located in the old city, on an ancient hilltop. Rehearsal took place in the converted great room of a 15th century church around the corner from the theatre, where due to the absence of windows wide wood doors were left open to let the sun and air stream in. Class began at 10:00 and for two hours it was shaded and cool and the music from the out of tune piano was interrupted only by the occasional squeak of the clothesline next door where the hotel chambermaid was hanging laundry. As noon approached and sweat steadily beaded our leotards, the climate outside changed and along with the sun and air into our medieval studio came heat and wafts of fragrant olive oil, sizzling garlic and onions. By 1:00 the sound of a frappé evoked images of smooth and elastic dough slapping on heavy stone slabs. Muscles in pointe shoes were kneaded and stretched in musical rhythm with the thumping of the baker as he plied and massaged his dough. By 2:00 the afternoon siesta had begun, and we were ready for the trattoria. Nothing overpowers the sweet and heavy smell of a room full of dancers energetically chasing Tchaikovsky's notes like the perfume of fresh basil and Italian tomatoes bubbling under mozzarella.

A pizza stone keeps dough crispy and speeds up cooking time. Make sure oven is fully preheated and cook pizza in the upper third part of the oven to prevent overcooking.

pizza dough:
1 package (2 ½ teaspoons) active dry yeast
½ cup + ¾ cup warm water (105-115 degrees)
pinch sugar
1 ¼ cups unbleached all-purpose flour
¼ cup white cornmeal
1 teaspoon salt
1 ½ tablespoons olive oil
1 teaspoon white cornmeal
olive oil cooking spray

Sprinkle yeast over ½ cup warm water in a large mixing bowl. Let sit 5 minutes until foamy. Add flour, cornmeal, salt, and olive oil and remaining ¾ cup water. Mix together with a wooden spoon until dough forms a ball, then turn onto a lightly floured board and knead until smooth and elastic, about 10 minutes, adding more flour if necessary while kneading. Spray a bowl with olive oil then add dough and turn to coat on all sides. Cover bowl with plastic wrap then a damp towel and let rest in a warm place until dough doubles, about 45 minutes.
When dough has doubled, punch down dough and let rest 10 minutes. Roll dough into 1 circle for 1 large or 4 circles for individual pizzas.

marinara sauce:
1 teaspoon olive oil
1 medium onion, chopped
2 cloves garlic, minced
1 (28 oz.) can whole Italian tomatoes in sauce
1 tablespoon balsamic vinegar
pinch sugar
½ teaspoon salt
freshly ground black pepper to taste

Heat oil in a large non-stick pot over medium heat. Add onions and garlic, turn heat down slightly and cover. Let cook 5 minutes, until onions are soft. Add undrained can tomatoes, balsamic vinegar, sugar, salt, and pepper to taste. Simmer 30 minutes.

topping:
8 oz. shredded low-fat part skim mozzarella
2 tablespoons shredded fresh parmesan cheese
2 tablespoons fresh chopped oregano or basil leaves
¼ teaspoon crushed red pepper, optional
1 teaspoon drained capers
1 tomato, thinly sliced
¼ red onion, thinly sliced

Preheat oven to 500 degrees. Sprinkle baking pan or pizza stone with 1 teaspoon white cornmeal and slide prepared dough onto pan. Spread marguerita sauce over center of dough and cover with remaining toppings. Bake about 10 minutes, or until edges of dough begin to brown and cheese is bubbly.

curried banana balls with masoor daal

The inspiration for this recipe came from the kitchen of my world-class bird-watching friends Drs. Dodgie and Lorna Engelman, who whipped up a vegetarian feast for my friends and me each night during a visit to their jungle retreat a few miles from the Panama Canal. Boiled unripe bananas make an unusual base for these tasty 'meatballs', which are served in a purée of cumin-spiced red split lentils (masoor daal) for a rich vegetarian stew that can be served on its own or as a side dish for chicken tandoori or grilled meats. Use only very green bananas as the sugar content of ripened fruit make them unsuitable for this recipe.

Serves 4

1 ½ lbs. unpeeled unripe green bananas
2 tablespoons vegetable oil, separated
1 medium onion, finely chopped
1 inch piece fresh peeled gingeroot, shredded
1 clove garlic, finely chopped
½ teaspoon salt
pinch cayenne pepper
¼ teaspoon chili powder
1 teaspoon ground cumin
1 teaspoon ground coriander
¼ teaspoon ground turmeric
1 egg, beaten

masoor daal:
2 cups red split lentils (masoor daal)
½ teaspoon turmeric
6 ½ cups water
1 tablespoon vegetable oil
½ teaspoon kalonji seeds (optional)
1 dried red chile
2 teaspoons vegetable oil
1 medium onion, sliced
½ hot red or green chili, seeded and finely chopped
1 ½ teaspoons salt
1 tablespoon lime or lemon juice

Prepare banana balls first. Bring a large pot of water to a rolling boil. Add bananas in their peels and cook approximately 10 minutes, or until peels begin to split. Remove bananas and let cool, then peel and mash well. Set aside.

Heat 1 tablespoon oil in a large sauté pan over medium heat. Add onions and ginger and cook over medium heat until soft. Add garlic and cook one minute longer, then stir in mashed banana, salt, cayenne, chili powder, cumin, and coriander and mix well. Cook, stirring and mashing with a wooden spoon for another 5 minutes over low heat. (mixture should be fairly dry) Remove from heat and let cool. Mix in beaten egg then shape into 10-12 "meatballs". Set aside while you prepare the daal.

Prepare lentil sauce: Bring 6 ½ cups water to a boil. Add lentils and turmeric and simmer, covered, over medium heat for 15 minutes, or until lentils are tender.

In another small pan, heat 1 tablespoon vegetable oil over medium-high heat. Add kalonji seeds and red chile and cook about 5 seconds, or until chile turns a few shades darker. Add onion and fry, stirring often, until nicely caramelized, about 15 minutes. Remove dried chile. Stir in green chili and sauté 2 minutes more. Stir in cooked lentils along with salt and lime or lemon juice. Keep warm.

To serve: Spray a large non-stick skillet with remaining 1 tablespoon vegetable oil and place over medium heat. Add banana balls and fry until lightly browned on all sides. Divide lentil purée (daal) among bowls and top with banana balls. Serve straight away.

curried banana balls with masoor daal

crêpes ratatouille

This simple Provençal vegetable stew makes a wonderful filling for crêpes. They make a good accompaniment to both simple light dishes such grilled fish or a saffron-scented bouillabaisse or a more hearty rosemary and lemon roasted chicken. Or skip the crêpes altogether and serve the ratatouille as a sauce for spaghetti.

Serves 4

non-fat crêpes:
2 egg whites
1 teaspoon sugar
1/3 cup non-fat milk
¼ teaspoon salt
½ cup all-purpose flour
1/3 cup water
vegetable oil cooking spray

ratatouille:
1 medium eggplant, cut lengthwise into ½ inch slices
½ green bell pepper, seeded and halved
1 red bell pepper, seeded and halved
1 medium zucchini, cut in half lengthwise
1 yellow squash, trimmed and cut in half lengthwise
1 large onion, cut in half
4 cloves garlic, peeled and chopped
1 teaspoon olive oil
1 tablespoon tomato paste
3 tablespoons dry white wine
1 teaspoon dried oregano or basil leaves
1 teaspoon ground thyme
1 tablespoon capers
1 bay leaf
salt and freshly ground pepper
vegetable oil cooking spray
parmesan cheese, optional

Preheat broiler.

For the crêpes: Whisk together egg whites and non-fat milk until well blended. In a small mixing bowl combine flour, sugar, and salt, then sift over the egg white mixture. Stir to blend, then add remaining 1/3 cup water and continue whisking until batter is smooth. Let stand 30 minutes.

Place eggplant, bell peppers, zucchini, squash, sliced onion and garlic cloves in a single layer on a baking sheet and spray tops lightly with oil. Broil until lightly charred then turn vegetables over and repeat on other side. Let cool then cut into large dice. Set aside.

Heat oil In a medium pot. Add tomato paste and sauté for 2 minutes over medium high heat. Add vegetables, wine, and herbs and simmer over low heat for 10 minutes. Season with salt and pepper.

Spray an 8-inch non-stick skillet or crêpe pan with cooking spray and place over medium-high heat. When pan is hot, add ¼ cup batter to center of pan, then quickly tilt pan in a circular motion to evenly distribute batter in a circle. Let cook 20-30 seconds until edges begin to brown, then loosen with a spatula and flip to other side. Cook another 20 seconds then transfer to a heated plate. Repeat with remaining batter, placing a sheet of wax paper between each crêpe.

To serve: Remove ratatouille from oven and discard bay leaf. Spoon about ½ cup ratatouille across the middle of each crêpe. Wrap sides over and place folded ends down on a plate. Sprinkle with parmesan cheese and serve.

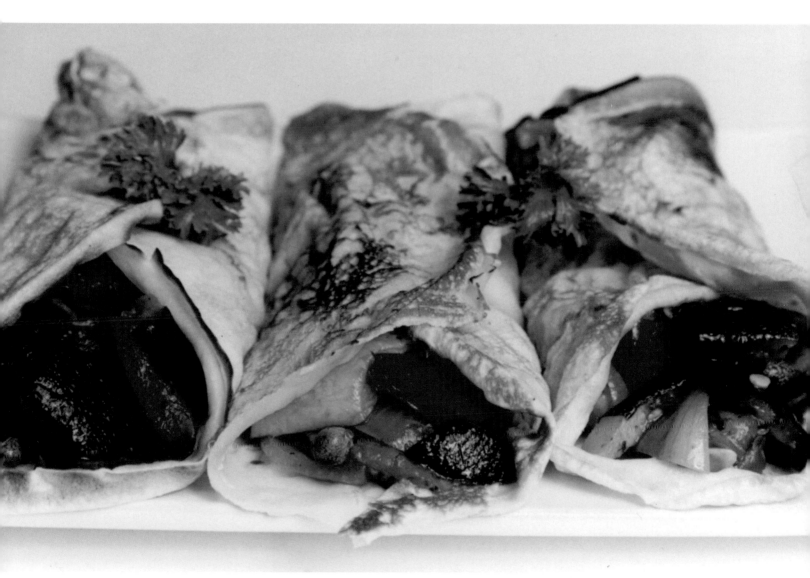

crêpes ratatouille

southwestern black bean and polenta burritos with fresh tomato salsa

The amounts of the ingredients in these low-fat burritos are only a guide. Feel free to add a little more cheese or less onions, or substitute different types of beans, rice, or cheese. Try white cannellini beans with mozzarella and minced sun-dried tomatoes or kidney beans with brown rice and green tomato salsa.

Serves 4-6

1 teaspoon vegetable oil
1 small onion, finely chopped
½ green bell pepper, seeded and chopped
½ jalapeno pepper, seeded and finely minced
1 (15½ oz.) can black beans, drained and rinsed
½ teaspoon ground coriander
½ teaspoon ground cumin
salt and freshly ground black pepper
vegetable oil cooking spray
1 lb. prepared polenta, plain or with sun-dried tomatoes, sliced ½ inch thick
4-6 flour tortillas
1 (14oz.) jar salsa
1 ½ cups cooked brown rice, optional
4 oz. low-fat or fat-free monterey jack cheese, shredded
4 oz. low-fat or fat-free cheddar cheese, shredded
fresh tomato salsa (recipe follows)
1 fresh ripe avocado, sliced
½ cup fat-free sour cream, optional

Preheat oven to 400 degrees.
Sauté onions, bell pepper, and jalapeno in oil about 5 minutes,or until soft. Add coriander, cumin, and black beans and cook until heated through. Season with salt and freshly ground black pepper and keep warm.
Spray another frying pan with vegetable oil cooking spray. Fry polenta in a single layer over medium heat until light and golden on both sides.

Layer black beans, brown rice, and polenta in the center of each tortilla, then top with cheeses and a few tablespoons of salsa.
Roll each tortilla in a cylinder and place side by side in a large glass casserole dish. Bake 15 minutes or until heated through (or microwave to heat through). Garnish with sliced avocado, sour cream, and fresh tomato salsa.

fresh tomato salsa

2 ripe fresh tomatoes, diced
½ cup cooked corn
3 tablespoons chopped fresh cilantro leaves
¼ teaspoon salt
½ fresh green chile, finely minced
1 tablespoon red wine vinegar

Combine all ingredients in a bowl and let sit 10 minutes. Spoon over hot burritos.

À la seconde...(side dishes)

georgia sweetcorn pudding

This savory egg custard was my initiation to southern food, which I first tasted during a guesting at the Grand Opera House in Macon, Georgia. I make it a little lighter with extra egg whites, compromising its authenticity to make it taste more like a dense corn soufflé. It makes a nice side dish for Thanksgiving.

Serves 6

1 cup low-fat milk
1 egg
2 egg whites
1 (15oz.) can cream-style corn
1/3 cup seasoned breadcrumbs
1 tablespoon vegetable oil
2 teaspoons sugar
2 tablespoons finely chopped onion
½ teaspoon salt
freshly ground white pepper to taste
paprika

Preheat oven to 325 degrees. Heat milk over low heat until scalded. Whisk egg and egg whites then mix with cream-style corn, bread crumbs, oil, sugar, onion, salt, and white pepper. Mix well. Slowly stir in hot milk. Pour into a 6-cup casserole or 6 small soufflé dishes. Sprinkle top with paprika. Set casserole or soufflé dishes in a pan of 1 inch deep water. Bake about 1 hour for casserole and 35 minutes for soufflé dishes, until knife inserted in the center comes out clean.

italian fontina, parmesan and potato gratin

Serves 6

2 ½ lbs. Yukon Gold potatoes, peeled and thinly sliced
1 ½ cups low-fat milk
½ cup half & half
1 tablespoon flour
½ cup shredded Italian fontina cheese
¼ cup grated reduced-fat parmesan cheese
1 clove garlic, finely chopped
½ teaspoon salt
freshly ground black pepper
pinch nutmeg

Preheat oven to 350 degrees. Spray a large casserole dish (11 x 17 inches) with cooking spray and lay half the potatoes in a single layer. Sprinkle with the flour and garlic, then half the cheeses. Season with half the salt and a grind of black pepper. Top with remaining potatoes, then cheeses and remaining salt. Pour milk and half & half gently over the top and along the edges. Sprinkle with a little more pepper and a pinch of nutmeg. Cover with foil and bake 1 hour 10 minutes, or until potatoes are cooked through. Remove foil and place under a broiler until top is crispy. Serve hot.

cold sesame soba with tofu

Serves 4

3 bundles (12 oz.) buckwheat soba noodles
1 (10 oz.) box firm tofu, patted with paper
towels and cut into cubes
2 teaspoons sesame oil
1 teaspoon chili oil
4 medium scallions, thinly sliced
½ medium cucumber, peeled and sliced
1 tablespoon soy sauce
1 nori sheet

Cook soba noodles in rapidly boiling water 3
minutes. Drain and rinse with cool water then toss
with cucumbers, scallions, chili and sesame oil. Add
tofu and soy sauce and gently toss again.
Toast nori sheet over gas or electric burner just until
dry and crisp, about 5 seconds.
Divide noodles among bowls. Crumble nori sheet
between palms and sprinkle over noodles just before
serving.

thai coconut rice

*Coconut rice is usually boiled in full-fat coconut milk,
which makes a delicious, albeit heavy accompaniment
to grilled meats and curries. I use only as much coconut
milk as is needed for good flavor and enhance the rice
with a fragrant broth made with shrimp shells and
lemongrass.*

Serves 4

1 tablespoon vegetable oil
2 cups jasmine rice, rinsed in a colander
2 cups shrimp stock (recipe following)
¼ cup coconut milk
pinch sugar
1 teaspoon salt

Heat oil over medium heat in a pan with a tight-fitting lid. When oil is hot, add rice and stir to coat with
oil. Add stock, coconut milk, sugar, and salt and stir
well. Bring to a boil, then reduce heat to very low
and simmer until all liquid is absorbed, about
15-18 minutes. Stir again to fluff rice, then recover
and let sit off the heat for another 10 minutes. Fluff
again and serve hot.

shrimp stock

*This stock is a good way to squeeze great flavor out of
shrimp shells. It can be frozen in small containers to
add to stir fries and curries, or as a base for noodle
soup.*

5 cups cold water
½ medium onion or 2 shallots, sliced
1 stalk fresh lemongrass, cut into 2 pieces
1 inch piece fresh ginger, peeled
2 sprigs fresh coriander, optional
½ teaspoon salt
Shrimp shells and tails from 1 lb. raw shrimp

Combine all ingredients except shrimp shells in a
medium pot and bring to boil. Reduce heat and
simmer 20 minutes, then add shrimp shells and
simmer another 20 minutes. Strain stock and discard
shells and vegetables. Pour stock in a shallow pan and
boil to concentrate flavor, reducing about 25%.
Remove from heat and use immediately or cool stock
over a bowl of ice water then freeze for another use.

sweet potato mash with green chile and brown mustard seeds

Serves 4

3 large sweet potatoes
1 tablespoon vegetable oil
½ teaspoon black or brown mustard seeds
½ large green pepper, chopped
1 fresh green chile, finely minced
½ teaspoon ground cumin
1 tablespoon dark brown sugar
¼ teaspoon salt
1 tablespoon freshly squeezed lemon juice

Bake potatoes at 400 degrees until soft, about 40 minutes to 1 hour, depending on size. (Or microwave potatoes on high power until soft about 6-10 minutes.) Let cool, then split and mash the insides. Discard skins.
Heat oil in a pot over medium-high heat. When oil is hot add mustard seeds. Cover pot and let seeds pop 5-10 seconds or until popping sound dies down. Add peppers and brown sugar and sauté 3-4 minutes over medium heat, until peppers are soft. Add mashed potatoes and salt and heat through. Stir in lemon juice. Serve hot.

grilled zucchini with garlic and fresh thyme

Here's a great side dish you can make on the barbeque or under the broiler. It can be served hot or room temperature as antipasto, partnered with some roasted red peppers, slivers of pecorino cheese and lots of fresh Italian bread.

Serves 4

2 medium zucchini, scrubbed and sliced ¼ inch thick
¼ teaspoon salt
1 large clove garlic
2 tablespoons extra-virgin olive oil
3 tablespoons freshly squeezed lemon juice
1/3 cup loosely packed fresh thyme leaves
freshly ground black pepper

Sprinkle sliced zucchini with salt and set aside. Prepare marinade by slicing garlic into paper-thin slivers. Place in a large bowl with olive oil, lemon juice, and fresh thyme, reserving a few sprigs for garnish. Whisk marinade with fork. Add zucchini and toss well. Cover and marinate in refrigerator 1 hour. Heat grill, grill pan, skillet or broiler over medium-high heat. Remove zucchini from refrigerator and shake off excess marinade. Grill or broil slices in a single layer about 3-4 minutes on each side, or sauté in a pan until tender but crisp. Remove from heat and season with freshly ground black pepper. Serve immediately or at room temperature.

garlic mushrooms

This quick Spanish tapa tastes as good with a piping hot omelette as a lean grilled steak, which is how I first tasted them in a Spanish restaurant in London. The key is to sear the mushrooms over very high heat and use lots of fresh garlic.

Serves 4

1 lb. fresh mushrooms, quartered
1 jalapeno pepper, seeded and sliced
5 large cloves garlic, sliced
3-4 tablespoons extra-virgin olive oil
salt & freshly ground black pepper to taste

Toss mushrooms, jalapeno, garlic, and oil together in a bowl and let stand 15 minutes. Heat a non-stick wok over high heat for about 5 minutes. When very hot, add contents of bowl and sear the mushrooms without stirring for 1 minute. Turn heat down slightly and quickly sauté 2-3 minutes more, just until mushrooms are soft. Season with salt and pepper. Serve immediately.

grand jeté

Fifth

Center Stage

Entrées

Despite having the reputation of being starving artists, ballet dancers lead very rich lives. One of the perks of becoming a ballerina is being lucky enough to travel all over the world. For me, this was also a great opportunity to sample and savor one culinary adventure after another. From Marrakech to Galway Bay, to a little Umbrian town called Spoleto, the following recipes are a healthy repertoire of exciting tastes to keep your palate jumping and your weight down.

moroccan chicken tagine with preserved lemon

lemon spritzer

marrakech mint tea

madras chicken tandoori

indian spiced grilled chicken

lighter barbeque sauce with lemon and red chile

rock cornish game hens roasted with rosemary and lemon

lemongrass scented thai chicken curry

spaghetti with turkey and fresh tarragon meatballs

cappellini scampi

broiled wild salmon with fresh berry sauce

exotic fish tagine

sole and salmon twirls with maple glaze

grilled swordfish with corn and black bean salsa

seared sea scallops with french lentils and garlic oil

sea bass wrapped in pancetta

poached salmon with cucumber dill sauce

grilled tuna with orange and thyme scented white beans

pork tenderloin with mission figs and apricots

rack of lamb with ginger mint chutney crust

pepper steak

moroccan chicken tagine with preserved lemon

This simple one pot chicken stew with its heady lemon aroma and unusual taste makes an impressive main course for casual entertaining. The essential ingredient is in the preserved lemons, which only take a few minutes to prepare, but must be made several days in advance.

Serves 6

tagine:
4 lb. chicken
1 ½ tablespoons olive oil
2 medium onions, thinly sliced
6 cloves garlic, finely minced
1 inch piece fresh ginger, peeled and sliced paper-thin
2 pinches saffron
2 teaspoons caraway seeds
1 ½ tablespoons ground cumin
1 teaspoon paprika
¼ teaspoon cayenne pepper
2/3 cup warm water
¼ preserved lemon, chopped (see glossary)
½ cup fresh cilantro leaves
½ cup sliced black olives, optional
freshly ground black pepper

½ cup fresh cilantro leaves, for garnish

cous cous:
2 ¼ cups water
¼ teaspoon salt
1 box (10 oz.) whole wheat or regular cous cous
2 teaspoons margarine or butter, optional

Skin chicken and trim of all visible fat. Cut into pieces. Heat oil in a large pot. Add onion and cover. Sweat 3 minutes, then sauté over medium heat until translucent, stirring to prevent burning. Add garlic, ginger, and spices and sauté until aromatic.
Add chicken parts and stir to coat with onion mixture. Brown for 3-4 minutes then add warm water and preserved lemon. Cover pot and simmer 40 minutes over medium-low heat. If using olives, add during last 10 minutes of cooking.

Add fresh cilantro leaves and simmer 5 more minutes. Turn off heat and prepare cous cous.
To make the cous cous: bring water and salt in a medium pot to a rapid boil. Stir in cous cous and butter, if using, and cover. Remove from heat and let sit 5 minutes. Fluff with a fork before serving as a bed for the tagine.

lemon spritzer

Mint is said to calm the nerves, which is always a help for pre-performance jitters. This sparkling lemonade was inspired by a visit to a lively Moroccan restaurant located a few blocks away from Le Cordon Bleu in London. This special drink of lemon syrup, sparkling soda and lots of fresh ripped spearmint leaves goes great with tagines, especially in hot weather. Add a kick of vodka for a fresh cocktail.

Serves 4

½ cup granulated sugar
juice of one large lemon
½ cup water
1 liter club soda or sparkling water
1 bunch fresh mint leaves

Cook sugar, lemon juice, and ½ cup water over medium heat until syrupy, about 5 minutes. Let cool, then divide among 4 tall glasses filled with ice and several mint leaves ripped in large pieces. Top off glasses with club soda and serve.

moroccan chicken tagine

marrakesh mint tea

I met my friend Abida AbdellahfBen one balmy morning in the souk in Marrakesh as he was opening his tiny spice shop. He described the contents of hundreds of the little clay jars lined up on wooden shelves, then led me through the labyrinth of narrow streets to an even narrower one called El Hadada where his grandmother was rolling semolina for an authentic Moroccan cous cous. She handed me a tall glass of cool tea, steeped with large mint leaves picked from a plant in a heavy ceramic pot. I have made this tea the same way ever since, lining the glass with lots of fresh spearmint and sliced lemons.

Serves 8

2 quarts water
8 tea bags, preferably green tea, but you can use ceylon or orange pekoe leaves
2 cups fresh mint leaves
2 lemons, thinly sliced

Bring water to a boil in a large pot and turn off heat. Steep tea bags and 1 cup fresh mint leaves for 5 minutes. Strain tea. Divide the rest of the mint leaves among 8 glasses and add lots of ice. Pour tea into glasses, garnish with sliced lemon and serve.

madras chicken tandoori

Serves 4

2 lbs. chicken parts, rinsed and trimmed of excess fat
1 medium onion, chopped
4 cloves garlic, finely minced
1 tablespoon chopped fresh gingeroot, or 1 teaspoon ground ginger
3 tablespoons lemon juice
¾ cup non-fat plain yoghurt
1 tablespoon vegetable oil, optional
2 teaspoons curry powder
1 teaspoon salt
1 teaspoon chili powder
2-3 drops hot red pepper sauce
dash cayenne pepper
¼ teaspoon red food coloring

Place onion in a blender or food processor with garlic, ginger, and lemon juice. Process 10-15 seconds then add remaining ingredients except chicken and purée until smooth. Place chicken parts in a casserole dish and pour marinade over, rubbing into chicken parts with fingers. Marinate covered in the refrigerator several hours or overnight. Grill on barbecue or bake in 400 degree oven until chicken is cooked, about 40 minutes for bone-in chicken parts. If using boneless chicken breasts, broil about 10 minutes each side, or until cooked.

indian spiced grilled chicken

Yoghurt-based marinades are one of the healthiest ways to give poultry great flavor without adding extra fat. This recipe is also excellent for firm-fleshed fish such as swordfish, monkfish, or mahi mahi.

Serves 4

2 lbs. boneless chicken breasts, skinned and trimmed of excess fat
2 tablespoons finely minced garlic
1 2-inch piece fresh ginger, peeled and sliced
1 tablespoon water
½ teaspoon turmeric
2 teaspoons ground cumin
½ teaspoon sugar
¼ teaspoon salt
3 tablespoons plain non-fat yoghurt
lemon slices, for garnish

Place garlic and ginger in a small food processor and pulse a few times. Add 1 tablespoon water and process until mixture becomes a paste. (Or pound garlic and ginger with a mortar and pestle into a paste, adding only a few drops of water if needed.) Combine paste with turmeric, cumin, sugar, salt, and yoghurt. Mix well. Slash each chicken breast two or three times then add to marinade. Turn pieces well to coat with marinade. Cover and refrigerate several hours or overnight. Shake off excess marinade and grill on a barbecue, on a grill pan or under a broiler until done, about 10 minutes on each side. Serve garnished with thinly sliced lemons.

Blessing the theatre

Movement as dance has existed in India for thousands of years. It is believed to evoke magical powers in dancers which honor the gods, and the space in which the dance is expressed is considered sacred. Before the curtain opens, the stage and its surroundings must be blessed to safeguard against evil spirits which might affect the success of an artist's performance.

An Indian temple priest performs the ceremonial blessing on the center of the stage while the dancers gather around in a circle. The ritual begins with the burning of Sambrani powder to fumigate and purify the air. The priest then makes a paste of sandalwood powder and water and smears it with turmeric and vermillion, forming a cone as a symbol of Ganesha, the elephant-headed God and remover of all obstacles. He then recites verses from the ancient Aryan scriptures called the Vedas and the Upanishads to pray for the well-being of both performers and the audience. Next he cracks a coconut and lights a camphor, to symbolize the breaking of all obstacles. The performers then do namaskaram, the act of submission to the gods, by going on their hands and knees and take a blessing near the flame.

Many Indian recipes in this book were inspired by some of my classical Indian dancer friends working their artistry in my kitchen to celebrate the end of a collaborative dance tour between Ohio Ballet and the Bharata Kalanjali classical Indian dance company from Chennai, India. Let their pungent spices inspire and bless your own culinary performance!

indian spiced grilled chicken

lighter lemon barbeque sauce with red chile

Unlike thick and pasty bottled barbecue sauces, this lemon spiked sauce is light but potent and can be used on skinless chicken breasts or to baste turkey burgers.

½ cup bottled red chili sauce
1 tablespoon soy sauce
2 teaspoons worchestershire sauce
1 cup chicken stock
2 tablespoons freshly squeezed lemon juice
½ teaspoon salt
¼ teaspoon paprika
¼ cup unsalted light butter

Combine all ingredients in a small saucepan. Cover and simmer 10 minutes. Marinate chicken pieces in sauce 15 minutes, then baste often during grilling.

rock cornish game hens roasted with rosemary and lemon

This recipe was given to me by a street vendor in Morocco, a man with deep brown wrinkles and a live chicken dancing in a cage at his feet. He set up his one-man restaurant each evening at sunset in the center of the large square in Marrakesh, where competing fires lit up the night like theatre lights on Broadway. Each restaurateur enthusiastically cooked piping hot stews of spicy meats and roasted chickens on spits. I was told the secret to making a truly succulent chicken is to stuff the cavity with lots of fresh lemon and garlic, so the juices infuse the meat and keep it moist. The addition of balsamic vinegar produces a golden brown skin without basting with butter or oil.

Serves 6-8

2 cornish game hens, or 1 chicken
3-4 lemons
kosher salt
freshly ground black pepper
1 head garlic, with only half of the cloves peeled
6 fresh rosemary sprigs
½ - 1 cup balsamic vinegar, for basting

Preheat oven to 375 degrees. Clean chicken and cut off any visible fat. Pierce 2 of the lemons all over with a fork (or just 1 if using a chicken). Slice other remaining lemons thinly, reserving a few slices for garnish. Place hens or chicken in a roasting pan and place lemon inside. Thinly slice the peeled garlic cloves then stuff pieces, along with rosemary sprigs, under skin and inside cavity. Tie legs together with string. Brush tops and legs with ¼ cup balsamic vinegar, then sprinkle all over with salt and freshly ground black pepper. Pour ½ cup water into bottom of pan, then break up head of garlic and scatter along with lemon slices over hens and in roasting pan. Place in preheated oven and roast 1 - 1 ½ hours, basting every half hour or so with pan juices and rest of balsamic vinegar until chicken is cooked. Transfer hens or chicken to a serving platter and cover with tin foil. Let rest 10 minutes before cutting.

lemongrass scented thai chicken curry

Many Thai and Vietnamese curries are made with full fat coconut milk, making them heavy and high in cholesterol and calories. Of course that is also what makes them taste so good! This recipe uses far less coconut milk but remains rich and satisfying. If you don't want to take the time to make your own curry paste, find prepared green curry paste in Asian sections of better groceries. Serve over a mound of fragrant steamed jasmine rice.

Serves 4-6

curry paste:
1 tablespoon coriander seeds
1 teaspoon cumin seeds
2 shallots or ½ medium red onion, chopped
1 inch piece fresh ginger, peeled and sliced
2 cloves garlic, minced
1 inch piece fresh lemongrass, chopped
2-3 red or green hot chile peppers, seeded and finely chopped (depending on how hot you like your curry)
1 teaspoon shrimp paste (available at Asian markets)
3 tablespoons tamarind juice (see note below)
½ cup fresh coriander leaves and stems
1 green bell pepper, seeded and chopped
1 leek, white part only, sliced
¼ cup water plus 1 cup water
1 tablespoon peanut or vegetable oil

curry:
¾ cup low-sodium chicken broth
1 tablespoon Asian fish sauce
1 ½ tablespoons brown sugar
1 (15oz.) can reduced-fat coconut milk
2 lbs. skinless chicken tenderloins or breasts, trimmed of excess fat and sliced thinly
1 medium zucchini, sliced thinly
¼ cup drained bamboo shoots
½ cup frozen peas
1 large potato, cooked and cut into chunks
freshly ground pepper
3 tablespoons chopped fresh coriander leaves
¼ cup fresh basil leaves
cooked jasmine rice

Toast coriander and cumin seeds in a small pan just until they get a few shades darker. Let cool, then pound or process in a spice grinder to a powder. Mix with remaining curry paste ingredients except water and vegetable oil in the bowl of a food processor and pulse to chop, then process to a thick paste.

In a large pot heat vegetable oil. Add curry and stir-fry for 2 minutes, then add ¼ cup water and bring to a boil. Add remaining cup water and reduce heat. Simmer 30 minutes over medium-low heat. Let cool.

Combine 2-3 tablespoons curry paste with chicken stock, fish sauce, brown sugar, and coconut milk. Simmer over medium heat 10 minutes. Add sliced chicken, zucchini, and bamboo shoots and simmer just until chicken is done, about 5 minutes. Add peas and potato and cook 3 more minutes. Stir in coriander and basil leaves and serve over steamed jasmine rice.

Tamarind

is available fresh in pods or in blocks, usually from India or Thailand. I prefer the Thai kind, which has a firm caramel texture and is the color of molasses. To make tamarind juice, cut a 2-inch piece and place in a small bowl. Pour 1 cup boiling water over and mash tamarind down with a wooden spoon to incorporate as much of the tamarind into the water as possible. Strain the liquid into another bowl and discard the pulp.

Save unused curry paste by pouring into an ice cube tray and freezing. Transfer frozen cubes to a plastic bag. Cubes should each contain about 1 tablespoon curry paste. Use 1-2 cubes per 4 serving recipe.

spaghetti with turkey and fresh tarragon meatballs

A staple of every dancer's diet is pasta because it is quick, inexpensive and always good. These fresh tasting meatballs can also be made with lean ground veal or very lean ground beef.

Serves 4-6

meatballs:
1 ¼ lbs. lean ground turkey
1 recipe tomato sauce
2 teaspoons olive oil
1 lb. spaghetti or linguini
1 large onion, finely chopped
2 cloves garlic, minced
4 oz. fresh mushrooms, finely chopped (about 1 ¼ cups chopped)
¼ cup fresh tarragon leaves or 2 teaspoons dried
¾ cup bread crumbs or matzo meal
2 egg whites
½ teaspoon dried red pepper flakes
salt and freshly ground pepper to taste
1/3 cup all-purpose or wheat blend flour
olive oil cooking spray
½ cup chicken stock

Heat olive oil in a large non-stick skillet over medium heat. Add onions and sauté until soft, about 4 minutes. Add garlic and chopped mushrooms and cook until they give off their liquid. Continue cooking until liquid evaporates. Remove from heat and let cool.
Combine mushroom mixture and ground turkey in a mixing bowl. Add fresh tarragon leaves, bread crumbs, egg whites, red pepper flakes, salt, and freshly ground pepper to taste. Mix well with hands and shape into 12-14 meatballs.

Spray a large skillet with olive oil cooking spray and add meatballs in a single layer. Brown on all sides over medium-high heat, then add chicken stock. Cover pan and steam over medium-low heat until liquid evaporates, about 10 minutes. Transfer meatballs to pot containing tomato sauce (recipe follows) and simmer with sauce 10 minutes. Serve over hot cooked spaghetti or linguini.

tomato sauce:

2 teaspoons olive oil
½ cup finely chopped onion
1 tablespoon minced garlic
1 (28oz.) can imported tomatoes, chopped
1 (6oz.) can tomato paste
1 cup water
salt to taste
freshly ground pepper to taste
1 teaspoon dried basil leaves
¼ cup chopped fresh parsley
1 bay leaf
½ teaspoon dried thyme

Heat oil in a large pot and add onion. Sauté over medium heat until soft, about 3 minutes. Add garlic and cook 1 minute more.
Add remaining ingredients and stir. Mash tomatoes with a fork or potato masher if necessary. Bring to a boil then turn heat to low and simmer 30 minutes. Makes about 5 cups

*spaghetti with turkey and fresh tarragon
meatballs*

capellini scampi

Angel hair pasta makes a delicate bed for luscious garlicky jumbo shrimp. Be sure to use the freshest mozzarella and the best juicy ripe tomatoes you can find.

Serves 4

16 large shrimp, cleaned and butterflied (split lengthwise)
1 tablespoon extra-virgin olive oil
3 cloves garlic, finely chopped
¼ cup dry white wine
4 oz. fresh mozzarella cheese
2 tablespoons light butter
salt and freshly ground pepper

1 recipe tomato concasse:
½ lb. ripe roma tomatoes, peeled and chopped
1 clove garlic, finely chopped
2 teaspoons extra-virgin olive oil
salt and freshly ground black pepper
1 bay leaf
2 sprigs fresh parsley
1 sprig fresh thyme

1 lb. hot cooked angel hair pasta
1 tablespoon finely chopped fresh parsley

Place shrimp in a small bowl with olive oil and chopped garlic. Season with pepper and let marinate 15 minutes. Make concasse: Tie together the bay leaf, parsley and thyme. Heat 2 teaspoons olive oil in a skillet and add chopped peeled tomatoes, garlic and the herbs. Turn heat to very low and cook until most of the moisture has evaporated, making sure tomatoes don't burn, about 15 minutes. Discard bouquet garnis, season with salt and pepper and keep warm.
Heat 1 tablespoon olive oil in a large skillet over medium-high heat. Add garlic and shrimp and sauté just until shrimp turns pink, about 1 minute on each side. Sprinkle mozzarella over shrimp. Season with salt and pepper, then place under a broiler until cheese is melted.
Add butter to the same skillet, then white wine. Season with salt and pepper, cook 30 seconds, then spoon over shrimp. Broil shrimp until cheese is melted. Serve shrimp topped with tomato concasse over hot cooked pasta. Garnish with parsley.

broiled wild salmon with fresh berry sauce

Serves 4

½ cup thinly sliced scallions
3 tablespoons palm or brown sugar
3 tablespoons lower sodium soy sauce
1 cup orange juice
2 tablespoons white wine vinegar
½ teaspoon salt
¼ teaspoon ground white pepper
1 ½ lbs. salmon filets
2 cups fresh raspberries or sliced strawberries

Combine all ingredients except salmon and fresh berries in a bowl and whisk well. Add salmon filets and coat on all sides with marinade. Refrigerate for 20 minutes. Preheat broiler.
Reserving marinade, broil salmon skin side down about 12 minutes, or until salmon flakes when tested with a fork. Place reserved marinade in a small saucepan and cook about 5 minutes over medium-high heat until slightly thickened. Stir in berries and cook 1 minute more. Pour over salmon filets and serve immediately.

Peeling tomatoes:
Core and cut a small x into the base of each tomato. Bring a medium pot of water to a rapid boil. Fill another bowl with cold water and a few ice cubes and have ready next to the pot of boiling water. Drop in tomatoes and boil for about 5-10 seconds, or just until to see tomato skin begin to curl slightly where it was cut. Remove tomatoes with a slotted spoon and transfer immediately to the bowl of ice water. When tomatoes are cool, the skin will slip off easily. Cut in half to scoop out seeds.

broiled salmon with fresh berry sauce

exotic fish tagine

A tagine, or tagine slaoui, is an earthenware cooking pot used in Moroccan cooking that allows vegetables and fish (or meat) to simmer together in their own juices, flavored with a fiery spice paste called charmoula. If you don't have a tagine at home, a large ovenproof pot will suffice. In this recipe vegetables are simmered in the lemony broth, then the fish is added in the last few minutes to just cook through. The stew is then placed under a broiler to seal the top with a slight crust. Serve over a bed of cous-cous or with crusty bread to lap up the juices.

Serves 4

charmoula:
2 cloves garlic, peeled and minced
1 ½ teaspoons ground cumin
2 teaspoons paprika
¼ cup fresh coriander leaves
¼ cup flat-leaf parsley
2 whole dried red peppers, seeds removed and crumbled, or ½ teaspoon red pepper flakes
¼ cup fresh lemon juice

for the tagine:
2 lbs. fresh fish filets (any firm white fish such as cod, sea bass, monkfish, red snapper etc.)
2 large carrots, scraped and sliced
1 lb. ripe red tomatoes, seeded and sliced
1 small green or red bell pepper, cored, seeded and sliced
2 medium potatoes, peeled and cubed
1 large wedge preserved lemon, minced (see glossary)
2 cups fish or vegetable stock
1/8 teaspoon cayenne pepper, optional
2 medium zucchini, ends removed, washed and sliced

chopped flat leaf parsley to garnish

Several hours or the night before mash all the ingredients for the charmoula to make a paste. Rinse off fish and pat dry with a paper towel. Rub half (reserve other half for future use) of the charmoula on both sides of the fish fillets, then place in a casserole dish, cover and marinate one hour in the refrigerator.

Combine carrots, tomatoes, pepper, potatoes, preserved lemon, stock, and cayenne pepper in a tagine or large pot. Bring just to a boil, then cover and simmer 15 minutes over medium heat. Add zucchini and cook another 5 minutes. Slice fish into large pieces and add to the pot along with marinade and cook 5 minutes, or just until fish is opaque.

Drain the liquids from the tagine into a small saucepan. Bring to a boil over medium-high heat and boil until reduced by half. Pour reduced sauce back over fish and vegetables. At this point if you like you can place the tagine under a broiler to make the top a little crispy just before you serve it. Ladle onto a mound of hot cous-cous garnished with parsley and serve immediately.

sole and salmon twirls with maple glaze

If you can find wild salmon for this recipe its rich ballet-pink flesh will make a nice contrast against the white fish. Alternatively, buy the leaner cut tail end of farmed salmon.

Serves 4

1 ¼ lbs. salmon filets, skinned
1 ¼ lbs. filet of sole, snapper, or other mild white fish filets

glaze:
1 tablespoon butter
1 small shallot, finely chopped
1 clove garlic, minced
1 tablespoon finely chopped fresh rosemary leaves
¼ teaspoon red chile sauce
1 teaspoon balsamic vinegar
1/3 cup red wine
1/3 cup pure maple syrup
1 tablespoon arrowroot, dissolved in 1/3 cup water
salt to taste
freshly ground white pepper

steamed asparagus

Preheat broiler. Cut fish filets into long strips. Twist one strip of salmon with one strip of sole to make a rope, then secure ends with toothpicks. Repeat with remaining strips of fish, then place them on a lightly oiled baking tray.

Sauté shallot and garlic in butter over low heat until soft, about 2 minutes, then add garlic, rosemary, vinegar, wine, and syrup. Simmer about 3 minutes more, stirring, then add arrowroot dissolved in water and keep stirring about a minute more, until thick. Season with salt and pepper.

Baste fish generously with glaze. Broil 6-8 minutes, depending on the thickness of the fish, just until cooked through. Remove toothpicks and serve immediately. Goes well with steamed asparagus.

grilled swordfish with corn and black bean salsa

Serves 4

4 ears fresh corn or 1 ½ (15½oz.) cans corn, drained
1 (15 oz.) can black beans, drained and rinsed
½ fresh red bell pepper
2 scallions, thinly sliced
¼ cup fresh coriander leaves, chopped
3 tablespoons freshly squeezed lime juice
salt and freshly ground white pepper to taste
4 fresh swordfish steaks, about 6-8 oz. each
1 tablespoon olive oil

Preheat grill or broiler.
Combine corn, beans, bell pepper, scallions, and coriander leaves in a medium bowl. Stir in lime juice and season with salt and pepper. Let stand 30 minutes. Rinse swordfish and pat dry with paper towels. Rub steaks on both sides with olive oil and season with salt and pepper. Grill or broil 4 inches from heat for 4-5 minutes on each side, or just until cooked through. Serve immediately with corn and black bean salsa.

seared sea scallops with french lentils and garlic oil

Searing scallops so their edges crisp and insides stay tender requires two things. First, your pan must be piping hot, with no moisture. Secondly, try to find scallops which are not immersed in water because they will begin to release liquid as they are cooking in the pan and won't achieve the nice caramelization that locks in the flavor. Fresh sea scallops should be generous in size and creamy almond in color- if they're pasty white then pass them by. (Soaking makes them absorb more water, so they appear larger and weigh more). Just before you place them in the pan, dry them with paper towels, then roll lightly in olive oil. Have your spatula ready-- they only take a minute or two on each side to be perfectly cooked.

French lentils (also known as organic green puy lentils) are smaller than the brown variety and taste more delicate.

Serves 4

1 ½ cups green or brown lentils
4 ½ - 5 cups non-fat chicken stock
2 teaspoons olive oil
1 teaspoon butter
1 cup finely chopped onion
1 large carrot, trimmed, scraped and chopped
2 cloves minced garlic
½-1 small hot red chile pepper, trimmed and seeded and finely chopped
4 plum tomatoes, peeled, seeded, and chopped
salt and freshly ground black pepper
1 tablespoon lemon juice
2 tablespoons extra-virgin olive oil
1 clove garlic, smashed
1 lb. large sea scallops (about 12-16 scallops)

Rinse lentils. Bring 4 cups of chicken stock to a boil in a large pot and add lentils. Turn heat down to a fast simmer and cook lentils 30 minutes.

In another large sauté pan, heat 2 teaspoons olive oil and 1 teaspoon butter. Sauté onions and carrots over medium heat for 2 minutes, then add garlic, red pepper, and tomatoes and cook until soft, about 3 minutes more. Add cooked lentils and season with salt and pepper to taste. Heat through, adding ½ -1 cup more chicken stock, or just enough to make the lentils slightly soupy. Stir in lemon juice and keep warm.

Heat another pan until very hot, about 5 minutes over medium-high heat. Add 2 tablespoons olive oil and one clove smashed garlic. Press garlic down to release juice, then remove the clove just before it begins to burn. Roll dry scallops very lightly in olive oil and add to the hot pan. Let them stand one minute without touching, so edges form a nice crust, then flip over and cook 30 seconds more. Quickly spoon lentils onto plates and top with scallops. Drizzle a few drops of the garlic-infused oil left in the pan over the scallops and serve at once.

*seared sea scallops with french lentils
and garlic oil*

sea bass wrapped in pancetta

*In ballet, often less is more. Too much effort and the whole
picture looks forced, overdone. Arms in position, face
relaxed, not too much energy. A dancer must remember
equally what not to do. The same is true with fish-- keep
it simple and don't overcook it and you'll never go wrong.
Use a firm-textured fish in this recipe such as sea bass,
monkfish or even halibut, so it holds together in the
pancetta wrapping.*

Serves 4

**2 lbs. (approx. 4 fillets) fresh sea bass, skinned
3 oz. pancetta, prosciutto, or thin-sliced bacon,
cut into approx. 8 thin slices
freshly ground black pepper
1 tablespoon olive oil**

Preheat oven to 400 degrees. Lay 2 slices pancetta on
work surface so they don't overlap. Place one fillet in
the center. Season with freshly ground black pepper (no
salt- the bacon is salty enough), then wrap 1-2 slices
pancetta around each fish fillet. Secure with toothpicks.
Heat olive oil in a heavy pan over medium-high heat.
Add fillets and gently seal for about 1 minute on each
side, then transfer to a baking dish. Cover dish tightly
with foil and bake 10-15 minutes, depending on the
thickness of the fish, just until the fish flakes easily.
Serve immediately, garnished with julienne of leek.

*To give your dish height, make an easy garnish of julienne of leek. Cut a
medium leek in half lengthwise and rinse to remove any dirt or grit.
Dry well then cut into matchstick-size slices. Place on a baking sheet
and place in a 350 degree oven for 5-10 minutes, just until leeks begin
to brown on the edges.*
*Julienne of leek can be made several hours in advance and kept loosely
covered at room temperature for several hours. Crisp in a low oven for a
few minutes before serving.*

poached salmon with cucumber dill sauce

There is a pub in Galway on Quay Street called Ti Neachtin, built from the wood timbers of a medieval Celtic warrior ship. After a pint of Guinness, you can fuel up for an evening at a local ceili (pronounced kay lee; this is a celebration of Irish dancing) by standing in line cafeteria-style for a fillet of the freshest salmon you'll ever eat. Poaching allows the fish to cook through gently yet quickly, while retaining maximum moisture and the delicate flavor of its seasoned poaching liquid. This produces a butter-soft fish, cooked with no extra fat.

Serves 4-6

1 large salmon fillet (about 2 lbs.)
2 cups white wine
2 cups water
6 scallions, sliced
2 slices lemon
2 bay leaves
2 sprigs fresh thyme or dill
2 teaspoons dried dill weed
½ teaspoon black peppercorns
½ teaspoon white peppercorns

Combine all ingredients except the salmon fillet in a large saucepan. Bring to a boil over high heat. Reduce heat to medium-low, cover and simmer 15 minutes. Gently lower salmon into pan so poaching liquid is over and under fillets. Turn heat to very low and poach 5-10 minutes, depending on the thickness of the fillets. Check if done by slitting the center with a knife.
When salmon is opaque and flakes easily, lift out of liquid with a slotted spatula. Carefully remove skin with a knife. Transfer to a plate and cover with plastic wrap. Let cool to room temperature and serve with cucumber sauce.

cucumber dill sauce

1 large cucumber
¼ teaspoon salt
¼ teaspoon sugar
¼ teaspoon white wine vinegar
1 cup light or fat-free sour cream
3-4 tablespoons minced fresh dill
salt & freshly ground white pepper

Peel cucumber and slice in half. Discard seeds. Chop cucumber finely and toss in bowl with salt, sugar, and vinegar. Let stand 5 minutes. Fold in sour cream and chopped dill. Season with salt and freshly ground white pepper and refrigerate until ready to serve.

grilled tuna with orange and thyme scented white beans

Starving artists never go hungry when they work in restaurants. While I was training at Lincoln Center I used to work at a mediterranean café on Waverly Street in Greenwich Village and never had time to eat in between class and the beginning of my shift, so I would often get to the restaurant a few minutes early hoping for a taste of the evening's special. The grilled tuna over simmered white beans with thyme was one of my favorites and one of the best selling dishes.

Serves 4

1 tablespoon olive oil
1 large shallot, thinly sliced
2 (15oz.) cans great northern or cannellini beans, rinsed and drained
½ cup dry white wine
1 cup vegetable or chicken broth
1/3 cup orange juice
½ teaspoon honey
1 teaspoon dried thyme or 4-5 sprigs fresh thyme
1 tablespoon finely grated orange zest
salt and white pepper to taste
2 tablespoons chopped fresh parsley

4 fresh tuna steaks (about 6 oz. each)
½ teaspoon orange zest
¼ cup orange juice
2 teaspoons olive oil
½ teaspoon dried thyme

Heat 1 tablespoon olive oil in a large skillet over medium heat. Add shallot and sauté until soft. Add beans, wine, broth, orange juice, honey, thyme, and orange zest. Bring to a boil, then reduce heat and simmer 20 minutes, stirring occasionally. Season with salt and white pepper.
While beans are cooking rinse and dry tuna steaks. Combine ½ teaspoon orange zest, ¼ cup orange juice, 2 teaspoons olive oil, ½ teaspoon dried thyme, and pepper to taste. Rub mixture onto tuna steaks and marinate in refrigerator 15 minutes.
Heat grill or grill pan over medium-high heat. Grill tuna 4 minutes on each side.
Divide beans among 4 plates and top with grilled tuna steaks. Sprinkle with chopped fresh parsley and serve.

grilled tuna with orange and
thyme-scented white beans

pork tenderloin with mission figs and apricots

I like these fruity stuffed tenderloins because, unlike many of the fancy roulades I fiddled with at Le Cordon Bleu, these little porks look impressive with a minimum of effort. Just cut a slit down the center and tuck soft sweet mission figs and tart dried apricots inside, then tie to secure.

Serves 4

2 ¼ lbs. pork tenderloins
2 tablespoons butter, separated
1 medium onion, chopped
1 medium carrot, trimmed, peeled and chopped
1 stalk celery, trimmed and chopped
4 oz. dried black mission figs, sliced
2 oz. dried apricots, sliced
salt and freshly ground black pepper to taste
¼ cup sweet white wine
2 ½ cups mushroom broth
1 cup veal or lower sodium beef stock
1 inch piece cinnamon stick
¼ cup heavy cream

Preheat oven to 400 degrees.
Trim excess fat and silvery membrane from pork and discard. Trim about 1 inch off each end and reserve trimmings. Cut a slit along the center of each tenderloin, leaving a 1 inch margin at each end, to form a pocket down the center. (Do not cut all the way through the meat). Stuff each pocket with the mission figs and apricots and season with salt and pepper, then close pockets and tie with kitchen string to keep together just tight enough to keep the pockets closed. Set aside.

Heat 1 tablespoon butter in a large pan and brown reserved pork trimmings. Add onions, carrots, and celery and sauté over medium heat until well browned, about 10 minutes. Deglaze pan by adding white wine and scraping the bottom of pan with a wooden spoon to and cook until wine is reduced by half. Add mushroom broth and beef or veal stock and cinnamon stick and simmer over low heat 30 minutes.
While sauce is cooking, heat another large sauté pan with remaining tablespoon butter. Brown tied tenderloins about 1 minute on each side. Transfer to a baking rack and place in oven.
Cook 18-20 minutes, or just until meat is barely pink in the center. Remove pork from oven and cover loosely with foil, while finishing the sauce.
Pour stock for sauce through a fine strainer into another small pot and discard vegetables. Skim fat off surface by running a paper towel loosely over surface, then add heavy cream and simmer 10 minutes more. Season with salt and pepper.
Remove string from pork and cut into 1 inch slices.
Serve 4-5 pieces per person, with sauce spooned over.

rack of lamb with ginger mint chutney

Fresh mint chutney is a great partner for juicy pink little lamb racks. Buy the lamb with the bones already frenched (cleaned and bone white down to the eye of the meat) and this dish can be prepared in under 30 minutes, just make sure to rest the meat for a few minutes after you take it out of the oven so it will be nice and tender.

A raita or yoghurt sauce makes a good complement to these little lambs. Stir some chopped fresh coriander leaves and a dash of salt into non-fat plain yoghurt and serve alongside extra chutney.

Serves 4

2 lbs. rack of lamb with excess fat removed
1 tablespoon vegetable oil
freshly ground black pepper to taste

chutney: (makes about 1 cup)
4 cups fresh mint leaves
1 cup finely chopped onion
2 inch piece fresh ginger, peeled and chopped
3 tablespoons lemon juice
¼ teaspoon salt
1 teaspoon sugar
cayenne pepper to taste

Finely chop mint, onion, and ginger then mix with lemon juice, salt, sugar and cayenne. Let stand 30 minutes.

Preheat oven to 425 degrees.

Heat vegetable oil in a medium skillet over high heat. Sear lamb about 1 minute on all sides to seal, then transfer to a roasting tray. Bake 12-15 minutes for medium rare, or a few minutes longer depending on doneness desired. Remove from oven and cover loosely with foil. Let sit 5 minutes in a warm place before cutting. Slice shanks in between each bone to divide. Serve with chutney.

To french lamb shanks down to the bare bone, use a sharp knife and scrape the bones down so there are no bits of skin or fat. Bare bones will stay nice and white during cooking for better presentation on the plate.

pepper steak

Sometimes after a really strenuous ballet, nothing will do except a hunk of juicy steak, cooked medium-rare with mashed potatoes and garlicky pan-seared mushrooms on the side. This recipe is fairly rich though only a spoonful or two of sauce is needed for each serving. Prepared demi-glace will work in a pinch, and is available in the soup and stock section of good gourmet shops. The pepper should be crushed coarsely: if you smash it too finely, you will be coughing throughout the meal. If your steak fillets are less than 1 ½ inches thick, reduce the amount of pepper so it doesn't become overpowering.

4 fillet steaks, each about 4 oz.
1 ½ tablespoons black peppercorns
1 tablespoon olive oil
4 tablespoons brandy
2 tablespoons water
¾ cup veal stock or demi-glace
¼ cup light cream
2 teaspoons green peppercorns in brine, drained

Preheat oven to 425 degrees. Crush peppercorns coarsely with a rolling pin or the bottom of a heavy pan. I usually put them in a small plastic bag before pounding so they don't fly everywhere. Press crushed pepper into the sides of each fillet.

Heat a pan over medium-high heat, then add steaks and don't touch them for 3 minutes, so they can caramelize on the edges. Flip fillets to the other side and cook another 2 minutes. Keep pan for sauce. Transfer meat to a baking rack and place in oven. Bake 8-10 minutes for medium-rare or cook 2-3 minutes longer for medium steaks, depending on how you like your meat cooked. Remove steaks and let them rest in a warm place, loosely covered with foil.

Turn heat under pan to high. Add brandy and water. Rub bottom of the pan with a wooden spoon to scrape up brown bits. Cook just until brandy is almost evaporated then stir in demi-glace and simmer 2 minutes. Add cream and cook 2-3 minutes more over medium-high heat, then stir in peppercorns. Spoon over steaks and serve immediately.

pepper steak

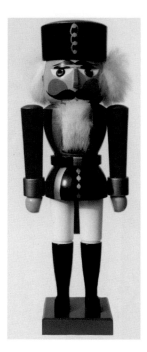

Nourishing the body and spirit would not be complete without a soul-satisfying sweet to complete a meal. The second act of the Nutcracker opens with The Land of the Sweets, the magical kingdom of the Sugarplum Fairy and her Cavalier, where decadent holiday goodies come to life. Nutcracker season begins shortly after Thanksgiving and continues well past Christmas, and even if you have never gone to the ballet, come January you will have heard Waltz of the Flowers as many times as a ballet dancer- in grocery stores, on the radio, and in television ads. From green grapes to new tires, it is probably one of Madison Avenue's most popular scores for December advertising, and Tchaikovsky's most well-known and best-loved work.

For most people the holidays mean time to celebrate with family and friends, to eat and drink too much and gain a few pounds. For dancers, the holidays can mean as many as fifty-four performances, and that's not counting rehearsals! Whether dancing on stage or just relaxing at home, recipes from the Land of the Sweets will suit any occasion. Angels food cake is a delicious fat-free base for fresh fruit or chocolate sauce. Show-stopping banana mousse pirouettes with warm caramel sauce elevate banofee pie to a new level, while luscious Triple Chocolate Polichinelles take chocolate truffles three steps further! Mother Ginger Cake, made with fresh gingeroot and dripping with sugar glaze, is perfect with afternoon tea. Legendary ballerina Anna Pavlova inspired the elegant Australian meringue dessert named after her. Try Quick-Steps for easy one and two step finales to your meal or to begin your day, including healthy blended smoothies and soothing cardamom-scented Chai tea.

phyllo wrapped poached pears with sweet red wine and orange syrup

Serves 4

1 cup red wine
¼ cup sugar
¼ cup orange juice
2 tablespoons lemon juice
4 bartlett pears, peeled and cored
8 sheets of phyllo, thawed
3 tablespoons butter, melted
2 navel oranges, peeled and segmented

Slice just enough off the bottoms of the pears to make a flat base. Combine wine, sugar, and juices in a medium pot and bring to a boil. Turn heat to low and add pears. Simmer for 15 minutes, gently turning pears often so poaching liquid coats all sides. Remove pears from pot and place on a dish to cool.

Turn heat up and boil poaching liquid down until syrupy, about 10 minutes. Set aside.

Preheat oven to 375 degrees. Cut phyllo into 8 squares measuring 8X8 inches. Place one square on a flat work surface and brush with melted butter. Top with another phyllo square. Blot the bottom of one cooled pear with a paper towel to soak up excess liquid then place on the center of the 2 sheets of phyllo. Gather edges up and twist around pear. Secure top with a piece of string. Lightly brush edges and sides with a little more melted butter and place on a baking sheet. Repeat with 3 remaining pears and phyllo sheets then place in oven. Bake 12-15 minutes, until edges of phyllo turn golden. Remove from oven and carefully cut off string. Serve immediately with a few spoonfuls of red wine syrup and peeled orange segments.

banana mousse

6 ripe bananas
¼ cup fresh lemon juice
1 envelope (2 teaspoons) unflavoured gelatin
¼ cup cold water
½ cup sugar
1 cup heavy cream
¼ teaspoon pure vanilla extract

Place bananas and lemon juice and process in a blender until smooth. Pass through a fine mesh strainer. In another small bowl sprinkle gelatin over cold water. Do not stir. Let sit 5 minutes.
Fold gelatin into banana mixture. Chill in the refrigerator about 30 minutes, until thick but not set. In another bowl whip chilled cream until soft peaks form. Fold gently into banana mixture. Chill several hours or overnight.

caramel sauce

1 cup sugar
½ cup water
½ cup heavy cream
2 tablespoons butter

Combine sugar and water in a small saucepan and place over medium heat. Bring to a boil without stirring. Watch carefully and brush down sides with a pastry brush dipped in water to prevent sugar from crystallizing and continue boiling until sugar turns deep caramel in color. (You can gently swirl the pan if sugar begins to color unevenly.) Remove from heat and add cream and butter. Don't worry if sugar seizes, it will smooth out after a few seconds. Stir until smooth.

To serve: Melt dark chocolate in a double boiler over very low heat (or microwave for 1-2 minutes until partly melted and stir until smooth). Line up pirouettes closely on a tray. Dip a fork into chocolate then shake across tops of pirouettes to form lines. Place tray in refrigerator until chocolate is set.
Fill a pastry bag with banana mousse and pipe into each pirouette. Place two pirouettes on each plate and surround with caramel sauce. Garnish with raspberries and mint.

banana mousse pirouettes with chocolate and
warm caramel sauce

light as air chocolate soufflé

You would never guess that this heavenly soufflé has less than 2 grams of fat per serving! Serve immediately as the soufflé begins to shrink shortly after removing from the oven.

Serves 6

2/3 cup high quality cocoa powder (preferably Dutch-process unsweetened cocoa powder)
¾ cup + 1 tablespoon granulated sugar
4 teaspoons cornstarch
1 teaspoon instant coffee granules
1 cup skim milk
2 teaspoons pure vanilla extract
7 large egg whites, room temperature
¼ teaspoon cream of tartar
dash salt
1 teaspoon finely grated semi-sweet chocolate
powdered sugar
vegetable oil cooking spray

Place oven rack on bottom third of oven and preheat to 350 degrees. Prepare a large soufflé dish or 6 individual soufflé cups by spraying with cooking spray then sprinkling with 1 tablespoon sugar over bottom and sides. Beat egg whites until foamy. Add cream of tartar and a dash of salt and continue beating until soft peaks form. Sprinkle remaining ½ cup sugar over top of egg whites and continue beating until stiff but not dry. Combine cocoa, ¼ cup sugar, cornstarch, coffee, and milk in a small pot. Bring to a boil, whisking constantly and continue to cook one more minute, until consistency of pudding. Remove from heat and whisk in vanilla. Let cool.

Stir cooled cocoa with whisk until smooth. Stir in ½ cup beaten egg whites then fold cocoa mixture with remaining egg whites. Pour batter into prepared soufflé dish. Sprinkle grated chocolate over top. Bake 25 minutes for one large soufflé or about 8 minutes for individual soufflé dishes. Sift 1 teaspoon powdered sugar over the top and serve at once.

spanish hot chocolate

Fargas is a little sweet shop in Barcelona which sells blocks of specially made chocolate with a spark of cinnamon that melts like velvet in hot milk. Spanish chocolate contains a high cocoa content, which gives a deep rich flavour. Godiva or Ghiradelli dark brand make the best substitute with a pinch of ground cinnamon added, although any good quality dark chocolate, milk or even white chocolate can be used in this recipe. If you prefer your chocolate sweet and milky, then try Swiss brands Suchard or Lindt, Belgian Leonidas, or Swedish Marabou.

3 oz. best quality chocolate
2 cups cold low-fat milk
2 tablespoons non-fat dry milk
pinch ground cinnamon, optional

Combine all ingredients in a small saucepan. Place over medium-low heat and slowly stir to melt chocolate until hot and smooth. Pour into two cups and serve.

triple chocolate polichinelles

Lower fat cream cheese adds creaminess with less fat to these luscious bon bons. Store them in the refrigerator and beware of their addictive effect-- too many and you may not be able to hide them beneath your skirt!

Makes approximately 24 truffles

1 ½ cups powdered sugar, sifted
½ package (4oz.) reduced-fat or neuchatel
cream cheese
5 oz. unsweetened chocolate
½ teaspoon vanilla extract
2 tablespoons Irish Cream liqueur (see note)
8 oz. premium dark or milk chocolate
2 oz. premium white chocolate

In a medium size bowl, beat cream cheese. Gradually add sifted powdered sugar, a little at a time, wiping sides of bowl with a spatula after each addition, and beat until light.
Break unsweetened chocolate into small pieces and melt over very low heat until almost melted. Stir until smooth, then add to cream cheese mixture. Stir to mix then add vanilla and liqueur and beat until well mixed. Cover with plastic wrap and chill until firm, at least 1 hour.
When chocolate mixture is firm, melt 8 oz. milk chocolate over simmering water. Remove chocolate mixture from refrigerator. Scoop out chocolate into small balls and place on a tray.

Drizzle melted chocolate over polichinelles to coat. Return tray to refrigerator until coating has hardened. Melt white chocolate. Remove tray from refrigerator. Dip a fork into melted milk chocolate and shake back and forth over truffles, making thin streaks over tops of each truffle. Return tray to refrigerator to chill until set. Store truffles in refrigerator or freezer.

Note: Other liqueurs may be substituted for the Irish Cream liqueur. Try Frangelico, Grand Marnier, or Crème de Cassis.

triple chocolate polichinelles

coconut flan

This variation of a classic egg custard is lightened with skim milk and sweetened condensed milk to take the place of heavy cream.

Serves 6

2 large eggs
3 large egg whites
1 cup skim milk
½ cup lite coconut milk
1 (14oz.) can low-fat or non-fat sweetened condensed milk
1 tablespoon pure vanilla extract
½ cup sugar
¼ cup water

Preheat oven to 325 degrees.
Combine eggs and egg whites in a large mixing bowl and whisk well. Add skim milk, coconut milk, condensed milk, and vanilla and whisk beat with electric beaters until well blended. Pour through a fine strainer into another bowl and set aside.
In a small saucepan, bring sugar and water to a simmer over low heat, stirring until sugar is almost dissolved. Raise heat to medium-high and cook, swirling pan once or twice, until syrup turns deep caramel in color, about 6 minutes. Remove from heat and pour syrup into 6 oven-proof ramekins or a 1 ½ quart size soufflé dish and swirl each dish around to coat bottom and sides.

Whisk egg batter a couple times then gently pour into coated ramekins or soufflé dish and place into a large pan filled with water deep enough to reach halfway up the sides of flan-filled dish. Place in oven and bake one hour for 6 ramekins and 70 minutes for large soufflé dish, or until outer edges are set. (Center should wiggle slightly when pressed with finger.) Transfer ramekins or soufflé dish to a rack and cool to room temperature, then cover with plastic wrap and refrigerate several hours or overnight.
To serve, gently slide a knife around edge of flan and invert onto a dish. Spoon caramel sauce over top.

coconut flan

pistachio biscotti

Crunchy and not too sweet, biscotti are easy when made with a food processor. They keep several weeks stored in a cookie tin. To make them a little more decadent, dip cooled biscotti into melted white or dark chocolate and chill on wax paper until set.

Makes about 20 biscotti

1 ¾ cups all-purpose flour
1 teaspoon baking powder
¼ teaspoon salt
¾ cup + 1 tablespoon granulated sugar
4 tablespoons (½ stick) sweet unsalted butter, chilled and cut into small pieces
1 cup shelled pistachios, coarsely chopped
3 large egg whites
1 teaspoon vanilla extract

Preheat oven to 350 degrees. Combine flour, baking powder, salt, and ¾ cup sugar in the bowl of a food processor. Pulse the machine once or twice to mix. (Or stir together flour, baking powder, salt, and ¾ cup sugar in a bowl. Cut butter in with a knife and fork or pastry blender until mixture resembles coarse meal. Skip next step.) Add chilled butter and pulse machine on and off until mixture looks like coarse crumbs. Beat the egg whites and vanilla together lightly, then pour over the dough all at once. Pulse or mix with large spoon just until a dough is formed. Transfer to a heavily floured surface and knead in nuts. Knead dough into a ball then form into a wide flat log, about 1 foot long. Place log on an ungreased baking sheet. With a sharp knife, make cuts crosswise along top, about ½ inch deep, so biscotti will be easier to cut after it is baked.
Sprinkle top with the remaining 1 tablespoon sugar. Bake 25 minutes, then take baking sheet out of oven. Let rest for 15 minutes, then cut log into slices and place biscotti on their sides on the baking sheet. Return to oven and bake 10 minutes. Turn biscotti over and bake 5-7 minutes more, or until edges turn golden. Remove from oven and cool on racks.

Variation: For almond or hazelnut biscotti replace pistachios with 1 cup slivered almonds or 1 cup coarsely chopped hazelnuts and 1 teaspoon almond extract for the vanilla extract.

biscotti di regina
(queen's cookies)

Makes about 3 dozen

6 tablespoons stick light butter, melted
1 large egg
1 ½ teaspoons vanilla extract
1 ½ cups all-purpose flour
2/3 cup sugar
1 tablespoon baking powder
½ cup sesame seeds

Preheat oven to 350 degrees. Whisk together melted butter, egg, and vanilla extract. Set aside.
In a medium bowl stir flour, sugar, and baking powder together. Add butter mixture and mix well with hands to form a dough. Pat dough into a flat log and cut into 2x1 inch pieces. Spread sesame seeds onto a plate and press each piece of dough to coat seeds on all sides. Place biscotti onto an ungreased non-stick baking sheet about 1 inch apart. Bake about 18 minutes, or until crisp and golden on the edges. Remove from oven and rest 1 minute, then transfer to racks to cool completely.

biscotti di regina

pavlova

This light Australian meringue dessert resembling the pillowy layers of tulle in a ballerina's tutu was created in honor of the famous early 20th century ballerina Anna Pavlova, who toured extensively and introduced ballet to audiences around the world. She was known for her poetic style of dancing traditional Russian ballets, especially her interpretation of the classic role of the Dying Swan. Make this luscious finale in dry weather as the meringues tend to get soft in high humidity.

6-8 servings

1 recipe meringues (following)
3 ½ cups fresh berries (a mixture of strawberries, blackberries, raspberries)
¼ cup Cointreau or Grand Marnier
¼ cup granulated sugar
1 cup heavy whipping cream

meringue:
6 large egg whites, room temperature
1 teaspoon fresh lemon juice
½ teaspoon vanilla extract
1 cup superfine sugar
1 ½ tablespoons cornstarch

powdered sugar, for garnish

Preheat oven to 375 degrees.

Combine egg whites, lemon juice, and vanilla in a medium-size bowl. Whip with electric beaters on low speed ½ minute, then on high speed for another minute until soft peaks form. With beaters still running, slowly sprinkle sugar over egg whites, ¼ cup at a time, and whip until glossy peaks form, about 2 minutes.

Shake cornstarch through a sifter over top of meringue and gently fold in with a rubber spatula. Drop 12 dollops of meringue onto a wax paper lined baking sheet. Place in preheated oven and immediately reduce temperature to 175 degrees. Bake about 1 hour 15 minutes, or until crisp on the outside and soft like marshmallow on the inside. (Test by lifting one carefully off baking sheet with a metal spatula and pressing bottom with finger.)

Remove from oven and let sit one minute, then lift each cloud off baking sheet carefully with spatula and let cool completely on racks.

Thirty minutes before serving: Place berries, liqueur, and sugar in a small bowl. Stir and let stand until serving. Whip heavy cream in another bowl to soft peaks.

To serve: Fill each Pavlova with a few spoonfuls of berry mixture and whipped topping. Sift powdered sugar over top and serve immediately.

To speed up whipping time put the cream in a stainless steel bowl along with the beaters and chill for 30 minutes before beating.

pavlova

mother ginger cake
with sugar glaze

Mother Ginger swaggers out of the wings in a cloud of face powder and a large balloon skirt that conceals her polichinelle children. In most Nutcracker productions it is actually a man who dons the bright pompadour wig and stilts to bring this popular character to life. With a flutter of her eyelashes and a wave of her fan, little polichinelles cling together around her legs, waiting for the moment they will burst out of the skirt folds to surprise the audience with an acrobatic dance of jumps and turns.

This exquisite cake is simple and yet still sophisticated, spiced with fresh ginger to taste both sweet and savory. The powdered sugar glaze is naturally fat-free and easy to prepare.

Makes 2 large loaves

cake:
½ cup (1 stick) sweet unsalted butter
4 oz. fresh ginger, peeled and finely shredded
¾ cup dark brown sugar
¾ cup dark molasses
2 eggs, lightly beaten
2/3 cup non-fat plain yoghurt
½ teaspoon salt
2 teaspoons baking soda
1 cup whole wheat flour
1 cup all-purpose flour
1 cup cake flour
½ cup low-fat buttermilk
icing:
2 cups granulated sugar
1/8 teaspoon cream of tartar
1 cup hot water
½ teaspoon vanilla extract
1 ½ cups powdered sugar

Preheat oven to 350 degrees. In a large mixing bowl, cream together butter and ginger until light and fluffy. Add dark brown sugar, molasses, eggs, and yoghurt and blend well.

In a separate bowl, sift together salt, baking soda, and flours. Add to batter alternately with buttermilk. Mix well. Pour into 2 large non-stick or greased loaf pans and bake 35-40 minutes, or until a knife inserted in the center comes out clean. Let cakes cool on racks.

To make the icing, combine granulated sugar, cream of tartar, and water in a small pan. Heat over medium-high heat to a thin syrup (226 degrees). Remove from heat and let cool. Stir in vanilla. Gradually beat in powdered sugar until the icing is smooth and pours easily. Drizzle icing to taste over the cake just before serving.

mother ginger cake

angels strawberry cream cake

This light angel food cake is simple enough for everyday, with a generous pouring of chocolate or gooey caramel sauce or dressed up for an occasion with fresh fruit and whipped cream or a fruit coulis made by tossing some lovely ripe ruby-colored berries into a blender along with a spoonful or two of sugar, and processing until smooth. If you're using raspberries you might want to press the coulis through a sieve to remove the seeds, though with strawberries, this step isn't necessary.

Serves 8

cake:
12 egg whites, room temperature
½ teaspoon vanilla extract
¼ teaspoon almond extract
1½ teaspoons cream of tartar
½ cup granulated sugar
1 cup cake flour, sifted
¾ cup superfine sugar
2 cups thawed frozen raspberries
4 cups mixed fresh fruit (strawberries, blueberries, kiwi, raspberries, peaches, black-berries)
1 tablespoon sugar
½ teaspoon vanilla extract
1 cup heavy cream

Preheat oven to 375 degrees. In a large bowl, beat egg whites until foamy. Add cream of tartar, vanilla, and almond extracts. Gradually add ½ cup granulated sugar a few tablespoons at a time and continue to beat until egg whites are stiff but still moist.

Sift flour and superfine sugar together over the egg whites ¼ cup at a time, gently folding in with a spatula until incorporated. Spray 8 mini bundt pans or 12 cupcake tins with vegetable oil cooking spray and fill with batter. Bake 15-18 minutes, until cakes are golden around the edges. Let cool until easy to handle then remove cakes from pans and cool completely on racks.

Make a simple berry coulis by placing thawed frozen raspberries in a blender and processing to a puree. Transfer to a fine sieve and press puree through to remove seeds. (Wipe bottom of sieve often with spatula so puree can go through more easily.) Discard seeds and stir coulis until smooth. (You can add a spoonful or two of sugar if desired. Stir into coulis until dissolved) Cover with plastic and chill until serving.

Make whipped cream shortly before serving: Place whipped cream in a bowl and place in freezer for 15 minutes. Remove and whip to soft peaks, adding 1 tablespoon of sugar gradually as you whip. Serve over cake, garnished with fresh fruit and raspberry coulis.

applesauce carrot cake

I used to stop at the Lincoln Center Coffee Shop every morning before class to pick up one of their incredible muffins; monstrous sized cakes that came in flavors like blueberries bursting out of dark bran and carrot-raisin, where you could actually see the shredded carrots and juicy raisins. It was a muffin the size of three ballerina buns put together. Since I no longer have Madame Tumkovsky's thirty-two grand battements to burn them off, I make this moist and delicious cake instead.

Makes 2 9-inch cakes

2 ¾ cups all-purpose flour
1 tablespoon baking soda
1 tablespoon cinnamon
1 teaspoon salt
1 teaspoon nutmeg
4 eggs
1 cup sugar
3 tablespoons vegetable oil
2/3 cup non-fat plain yoghurt
1 teaspoon vanilla extract
1 (15oz.) jar unsweetened applesauce
3 cups shredded carrots (about 1 lb.)
1 cup golden raisins, optional

Preheat oven to 350 degrees. Sift together flour, baking soda, cinnamon, salt, and nutmeg. Set aside.
In a large mixing bowl, beat eggs. Add sugar, oil, yoghurt, and vanilla and stir well. Add applesauce, carrots, and raisins and mix until well-blended. Fold flour mixture into batter just until moist and blended. Do not over-mix. Spray 2 nine-inch non-stick cake pans or 1 (12 x14 inch) casserole baking dish with vegetable oil cooking spray.
Pour in batter and bake about 30 minutes for 2 cake pans or 35 minutes for casserole dish, or until cake tester comes out clean. Let cool about 10 minutes in pan, then transfer to a rack to cool completely before slicing.

forbidden rice pudding

Glutinous Indonesian black rice gives this simple pudding a dramatic presentation, heightened by the contrast of bright green slivers of pistachio.

Serves 6

1 cup sweet black rice
5 cups water
pinch salt
¾ cup sugar
1 tablespoon corn starch
1 tablespoon water
1 teaspoon pure vanilla extract
½ cup lite coconut milk
¼ cup chopped pistachio nuts

Rinse rice well with hot water then place into a large deep pot with 4 cups water and pinch of salt and bring to a boil. Turn heat to medium and cook at a fast simmer for 40 minutes. Add sugar and remaining cup of water and cook over low heat 40 minutes more.
Dissolve corn starch in 1 tablespoon water, then raise heat to a boil and stir into rice. Cook, stirring, 2 minutes, then remove from heat. Stir in vanilla extract and ½ cup coconut milk. Let cool. Serve warm or at room temperature, drizzled with remaining coconut milk and sprinkled with chopped pistachio nuts.

forbidden rice pudding

irish soda bread

In Ireland, a large cross through the center of the dough serves both to allow the heat to penetrate the bread and, according to Irish custom, to bless it before it bakes.

Makes 1 loaf

3 cups flour
3 tablespoons sugar
2 teaspoons baking powder
2 teaspoons baking soda
4 tablespoons unsalted butter, cut into pieces
cup low-fat buttermilk (or 1 tablespoon apple cider vinegar mixed with 1 cup low-fat milk)
1 egg
1 cup mixed yellow and black raisins or currants
1 tablespoon caraway seeds

Preheat oven to 325 degrees.
In the bowl of a food processor, combine flour, sugar, baking powder, and baking soda. Pulse a few times to mix then add butter and pulse until mixture forms coarse crumbs. (Can also be made by hand: Cut butter into dry ingredients with a fork until mixture forms coarse crumbs.)
Whisk together buttermilk and egg then add all at once to crumb mixture and pulse or knead until dough holds together. Turn dough onto well-floured surface and work in raisins and caraway seeds.
Knead several times then form into a ball. Flatten top, then slash an X, ½ inch deep, across top of dough. Place on a non-stick baking sheet (or spray a regular baking sheet with vegetable oil spray) and bake 40-45 minutes, or until loaf sounds hollow when tapped and outside is lightly browned. Serve warm.

apricot banana bread

The natural sweetness of ripe bananas supplies most of the sugar for this healthier tea-time treat.

Makes 1 loaf

1 ½ cups all-purpose flour
1 tablespoon baking powder
¼ teaspoon salt
¼ cup brown sugar
3 medium mashed very ripe bananas (about 1 to 1 ¼ cups mashed)
2 egg whites
½ cup low-fat buttermilk
½ cup coarsely chopped dried apricots

Preheat oven to 350 degrees.
In a large bowl, combine flour, baking powder, salt, and brown sugar. Stir to mix thoroughly.
Add mashed bananas and remaining ingredients and stir with a fork just until combined. Do not over-mix. Scrape batter into a non-stick loaf pan or large muffin pans.
Bake 40-50 minutes, or until a cake tester comes out clean. Remove from oven and let cool in pan at least 10 minutes before slicing.

Quick Steps

Satisfy your sweet tooth in no time with these one and two-step ideas for easy desserts with minimal preparation, soothing hot drinks and refreshing blender shakes and smoothies.

macerated strawberries with balsamic vinegar

Some perfectly ripe juicy strawberries macerated in balsamic vinegar hit the spot on warm summer days. Sprinkle a few tablespoons balsamic vinegar and a teaspoon of sugar over berries and let sit at room temperature for 15 minutes. Spoon into small bowls and garnish with a sprig of fresh mint and a spoonful of whipped cream.

frozen grapes

A bunch of grapes tossed in the freezer for a few hours can transform an everyday fruit into low-fat low-calorie bite-size bundles of tart sweet grape sorbet! Rinse and dry red or green grapes on their stems and place in a bowl. Serve sprinkled with a few drops of calvados or poire william. Frozen grapes also make a festive substitute for ice cubes in wine coolers and summery iced teas.

chai

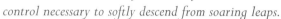

Maintaining good muscle tone is essential for professional athletes, however, unlike football players, ballet dancers cannot groan with pain or grunt on stage when they must expel maximum energy to perform their job. On stage appearance counts, and every step must appear effortless. Calcium, among its many vital roles, helps to maintain strength in the muscles, which helps to develop the control necessary to softly descend from soaring leaps.

This fragrant and calcium-rich tea is based on a traditional Bengal recipe, and can be brewed in the time it takes to make an ordinary pot of tea. Made with low-fat milk and whole cardamom pods, it is a soothing way to greet the day or add the final touch to an Indian meal. Decaffeinated tea bags can be used.

Makes 2 servings

1 ½ cups water
6 whole cardamom pods, slightly crushed
2 tea bags (preferably Darjeeling, but any black tea except Chinese tea can be used)
1 ½ cups low-fat milk
1 tablespoon sugar

Combine water, cardamom pods, and tea bags in a small pot. Bring to a boil, then reduce heat to low and simmer 5 minutes, until tea is strong and very dark. (Milk will be added to dilute tea, so make sure tea is darker than you usually brew.) Add milk and sugar and simmer 3-4 minutes, just to heat through. Do not boil again. Pour through a strainer into mugs and serve.

quick pear tart

Unlike butter-laden puff pastry sheets, phyllo dough contains only flour and water, which gives you license to drizzle a little extra butter.

4 sheets thawed packaged phyllo dough
2 sliced anjou or bosc pears
3 tablespoons butter
¼ cup dark or light brown sugar

Thinly slice pears and sauté in butter over medium heat until soft. Stack the 4 sheets of phyllo on top of each other and spread the pears down the center. Fold sides of phyllo over the pears and sprinkle with the sugar. Brush top with remaining melted butter from the pan. Bake in a preheated 350 degree oven about 10 minutes, just until edges begin to brown. Serve hot with vanilla frozen yoghurt or whipped cream. Serves 2.

grilled blood oranges and pineapple with orange flower water

After a spicy meal a simple dessert of grilled fruit takes the sweet edge off. Use blood oranges if you can find them, but they are just as delicious with ripe navel oranges. The light dusting of cinnamon gives them a Moroccan touch, which goes well after a lemony chicken or fish tagine.

Serves 2

2 ripe blood or navel oranges, sliced
4 slices fresh pineapple
¼ cup powdered sugar
2 tablespoons orange flower water
1 tablespoon mint leaves

Sprinkle oranges and pineapple slices with powdered sugar and place on a hot grill or grill pan and cook just until softened and lightly caramelized. Arrange on a dish and sprinkle with orange flower water. Garnish with thinly shredded mint leaves.

mango lassi

2 cups fresh mango, diced
½ teaspoon fresh ginger, finely grated
1 ½ cups plain low-fat yoghurt
1 teaspoon honey, optional

Place all ingredients in a blender, along with 6 ice cubes and process until smooth and thick.

pineapple-banana frappé

Serves 4

1 cup pineapple juice
1 cup chopped fresh pineapple
1 ripe banana
1 cup non-fat plain yoghurt
¼ cup canned cream of coconut
1 tablespoon honey
1 ½ cups ice cubes

Place all ingredients except ice cubes in a blender and pulse once or twice to break up fruit. Add ice and blend until thick and smooth, about 20 seconds. Serve in frosted glasses, garnished with sliced banana or pineapple.

glossary

Many of the recipes in this book contain foods that can be found in most good quality grocery stores. Asian markets are well worth the trip, and as most ingredients are bottled, dried, canned, or picked, they will keep for a long time in your pantry. If you don't want to go searching the aisles, check the listings under Websites and get what you need sent right to your doorstep.

Air popcorn popper- Munch through a whole bowl of air-popped corn for less calories and fat than even a few cups of regular oil-popped corn. Spray with butter-flavoured spray and a light sprinkling of salt.

Bamboo steamer- Inexpensive and available at Asian markets and kitchenware stores everywhere, bamboo steamers fit over ordinary saucepans and make attractive covered servers.

Black rice-A sweet glutinous rice with a nutty taste used in Asian cooking. Black rice can be purchased in Asian markets and gourmet stores and sometimes labeled as "forbidden rice."

Bulgar wheat- Sold in bulk form in health food stores and many supermarkets, nutty tasting bulgar is the whole grain of wheat dried and granulated into grain form.

Coconut milk- Available canned in the Asian or the baking section of supermarkets. Also look in the Mexican or Spanish food sections.

Chiles- Buy fresh red or green varieties, keeping in mind the heat level of different varieties. Always slice lengthwise and scoop out seeds with a knife before using.

Coriander- Also called chinese parsley. Cilantro is the leaf of the coriander plant and is widely used in Asian and Latin American cooking. Do not substitute dried or ground coriander for fresh leaves- the dish will lose much of the taste and texture and accent of color provided by the fresh leaves.

Eggs- To hard boil an egg place it in a small pot with a generous pinch of salt and cover it with cold water. Bring it to a boil then cook 10 minutes. Make a small crack with the back of a spoon, drain and cover with cold water. Let cool to room temperature. (The crack will make it easier to peel.)

Fish sauce- Called nam pla in Thai and nuoc mam in Vietnamese, fish sauce is the most essential ingredient in asian cooking. Fish sauce is made by draining the liquid off fermented salted anchovies. Both Thai and Vietnamese brands can be used interchangeably in any recipe calling for asian fish sauce in this book.

Fondue- This ballet term for a simple exercise of bending and straightening the knees with a melting motion at the barre helps to strengthen the legs and improve the elasticity of the muscles, so when warmed up, a dancer will appear supple and fluid, like good swiss gruyère.

Food Processor- Indispensible for chopping, slicing, shredding, mixing and for making smooth soups and sauces. I like the small cuisinart chopper for mincing garlic and ginger and whipping up small amounts of salad dressings.

Fouetté- The Black Swan pas de deux from Swan Lake made these whipping turns famous and a requisite feat for every professional ballerina. Use the same vigor when whipping egg whites and cream and for maximum volume make sure the bowl is very clean.

Frappé- In ballet, this step requires a brisk brush of the foot on the floor to promote sharpness and clarity in execution of movement. The french verb *frapper* means to hit, similar to the blade of the blender as it whips up the delicious yoghurt smoothies in the Quick Steps section of the dessert chapter.

Fresh food is infinitely more appetizing. If carrots have been sitting in your refrigerator for a month and have become flexible then they're not going to taste very good. If your onions or garlic bulbs are sprouting new limbs, throw them out.

Garlic- It's inexpensive, so buy it fresh and keep it on hand. Garlic powder is no substitute. Pickled garlic is sold packed in water in jars and sold in Asian markets (and doesn't give you bad breath).

Gingeroot- This knotty rhizome is widely available and should be kept in the refrigerator loosely wrapped in a plastic bag. To use, cut off desired amount and peel skin with a vegetable peeler.

Gravlax- This Scandinavian cured salmon "cooks" in an herbed bath of coarse salt and sugar over several days in the refrigerator. Make sophisticated canapes by slicing thinly on mini toasts with crème fraîche and a dab of caviar, jazz up hot linguini by tossing minced gravlax with some chopped fresh dill and a little cream, or serve with bagels and cream cheese for sunday brunches.

Herbs- Fresh herbs should be used wherever possible and can be kept longer in the refrigerator by standing stems upright in a glass filled with an inch of water.

Jasmine rice- More tender than other rice varieties, jasmine rice complements Thai curries with its delicate fragrance and is widely available in supermarkets.

Juicer- Nothing tastes better than freshly squeezed orange juice in the morning, unless it happens to be fresh carrot, cucumber, watermelon, mango, homemade lemonade, beet juice, green apple, fresh pink grape-fruit....

Kitchen scale- Keeps serving sizes in check and is useful for measuring bulk ingredients.

Lemongrass (citronella)- Fresh or dried, this tropical grass gives dishes an intensely fresh lemony flavor with a slight hint of ginger. Discard outer leaves and use the soft lower portion of the stalk, smashing slightly before chopping or slicing to release its aromatic flavour. Dried lemongrass should be soaked in warm water 1 hour before using (or buy it fresh and freeze in a plastic bag for later use). Use 1 teaspoon dried for each stalk of fresh lemongrass.

Mesclun- Baby greens mixture often with fresh herbs. May contain arugula, radiccio, escarole, chervil, frissé, dandelion leaves, and oak-leaf lettuce.

Miso- Made from fermented soybeans, salt and other grains and comes in white, yellow and brown varieties. Used to flavor soups, sauces and dressings. For the sesame noodle recipe in this book I use unpasteurized mellow white miso.

Non-stick pans- Make cleanup easier and reduce the oil and butter in your cooking.

Nori sheets- Pressed seaweed sheet for sushi rolls are sold the Asian section of supermarkets.

Oil cooking sprays- Olive oil, vegetable, canola, and butter flavoured sprays save hundreds of unnecessary calories. Use also for greasing pans evenly and easily.

Palm sugar- This syrupy thick sugar comes from the sap of the palmyra or sugar palm tree, and is sold in small glass or plastic containers in Asian, Indian and Hispanic markets. It is often used along with fish sauce and coconut milk to flavor Thai curries. If unavailable, use light brown sugar with a drop or two of maple syrup.

Poisson- This French word for fish is one of the most exciting movements in ballet, resembling its namesake by the position of a ballerina as she makes a diving leap into her partner's arms.

Preserved lemons- Preserved lemons are the key to Moroccan tagines. Fresh cut lemons lack the distinctive salty flavor provided only by using lemons that have been preserved in coarse salt. Although some recipes for tagines require lemons to spend up to a month in their salty bath, lemons for recipes in this book will sufficiently pungent after 4-5 days.

2 ripe lemons
½ cup coarse salt
½ - 1 cup fresh lemon juice

Cut 2 lemons into 8 wedges. In a small glass jar with a tight-fitting lid, pour ½ cup coarse salt. Place lemon wedges on top of salt and pour ½ cup or enough fresh squeezed lemon juice to cover lemon wedges. Cover jar tightly and sit in a cool dark place. Shake jar 2 or 3 times a day, to redistribute salt and juices, for 4-5 days. Store unused preserved lemons in refrigerator for 1-2 months.

Sauté- Both the culinary arts and classical ballet are joined by their common language, used both to denote cooking techniques and specific dance movements. Just as a sauté in ballet means a small jump from one or two feet, in classic cuisine this cooking term requires a deft hand to make food literally "jump off the pan", using high heat and little fat.

Sesame oil (toasted sesame oil) - Used mostly for adding flavor rather than for cooking, as it has a lower smoking point than other oils. Hot red chiles add a kick to spicy sesame oil, which is available in better gourmet grocery stores, but you can make your own by combining sesame and regular red chili oil, both of which can be found in the Asian section of most grocery stores.

Sesame salad dressing- I use Mitsukan brand to make my Japanese house salad dressing, but it can be hard to find. Alternatively, use any sesame dressing that contains whole sesame seeds.

Sesame seeds- Find black and roasted white sesame seeds in Japanese sections of the supermarket.

Shiitake mushrooms- These wonderful mushrooms have become increasingly available fresh but still have a wonderful musky taste in dried form. Soak dried shiitake in warm water for 30 minutes before using. Available in Asian sections of grocery and health food stores.

Soy sauce- Some recipes call for light or dark soy sauce, the taste and saltiness varying with the intensity of the color. I substitute low-sodium soy sauce as much as possible, especially in recipes where other ingredients containing salt are used.

Sushi rice- Sushi rice is a glutinous short grain rice, similar to the Italian arborio used for risotto. Its stickiness comes from the large amount of water absorbed during cooking, which is good for rolling inside sheets of nori for maki rolls or made into sticky rice cakes.

Tahini- Sesame seeds pressed to a paste give middle eastern dips their distinctive flavour. Find tahini (also spelled tahina) in Middle Eastern or Kosher sections of the supermarket.

Tofu- A good low-fat source of protein for those who do not eat meat, this versatile and mild tasting soybean curd can be used for meatless stir-fries, as a base for salad dressing, and even in cheesecakes. Sold in many varieties. Silken tofu is smooth and suitable for sauces and dressings. Soft tofu makes a wonderful vegetarian option for dairy-free puddings. Firm organic tofu tends to be denser and more meaty tasting, which works well in vegetarian stir fries. All varieties can be found in all health food or organic sections of groceries.

Turn-out- The foundation or technique of classical ballet is based on the rotation of the hips, legs and feet at a 90 degree angle to promote ease of movement in every direction. A ballet warm-up begins at the barre with exercises incorporating turn-out to stretch and strengthen the body. Warm-up can last up to an hour long, followed by an additional 30-60 minutes of exercises in the center of the room that employ balance, coordination and speed. As strength increases, the fluidity and control over quality of movement improves. Likewise with cooking, a chef must master the basics of *mise en place*, or preparation of ingredients, in order to create successful dishes.

Wasabi (Japanese horseradish)- Sold as a paste in ready to use tubes and in powder form. To use the powder form, just spoon a small amount onto a plate and mix in a few drops of water to form a bright green paste.

Web Sites- The internet makes shopping for unusual ingredients easy. Kitchen tools and gadgets can also be found with a virtual click. Try nisbetts.com, EthnicGrocer.com, homegrocer.com, farawayfoods.com, allindiagrocers.com and britsinthestates.com. If you have trouble finding any ingredient in this book, contact me at dancinggourmet.com.

Wok- Better than a frying pan because the shape allows the heat to be concentrated in the center of the pan, to keep vegetables crisp and juices sealed inside meat. Be sure to thoroughly heat dry wok by placing over high heat for 5-10 minutes before cooking.

Index

Conversion Chart

Equivalents for Imperial and Metric Measurements

The recipes in this book are given in Imperial measurements and have been geared towards an American market, but can be converted easily into metric terms. Use one or the other consistently throughout the recipe.

SOLID WEIGHT CONVERSIONS

US/UK	METRIC
1 OZ.	28 GR.
2 OZ.	56 GR.
3 ½ OZ.	100 GR.
4 OZ.(¼LB.)	112 GR.
5 OZ.	140 GR.
6 OZ.	168 GR.
8 OZ.(½ LB.)	225 GR.
9 OZ.	250 GR.
12 OZ.(¾ LB.)	340 GR.
16 OZ.(1 LB.)	450 GR.
18 OZ.	500 GR.(½ KG.)
20 OZ.(1 ¼LBS.)	560 GR.
24 OZ.(1 ½LBS.)	675 GR.
32 OZ.(2 LBS.)	900 GR.
36 OZ. (2 ¼LBS.)	1 KG.
3 LBS.	1350 GR.

LENGTH MEASURES (APPROXIMATE)

¼ in.	6mm.
½ in.	12 mm.
1 in.	2.5 cm.
2 in.	5 cm.
3 in.	7.5 cm.
4 in.	10 cm.
5 in.	13 cm.
6 in.	15 cm.
7 in.	18 cm.
8 in.	20 cm.
9 in.	23 cm.
10 in.	25 cm.
11 in.	28 cm.
12 in./1 ft.	30 cm.

OVEN TEMPERATURES

Fahrenheit	Celsius	Gas Mark
225	110	1/4
250	120	1/2
275	140	1
300	150	2
325	170	3
350	180	4
375	190	5
400	200	6
425	220	7
450	230	8
475	240	9
500	250	10

LIQUID MEASURES

FL.OZ.	US	UK	METRIC
	1 tsp.	1 tsp.	5 ml.
¼	2 tsp.	1 dessert spoon	7 ml.
½	1 tblsp.	1 tblsp.	15 ml.
1	2 tblsp.	2 tblsp.	28 ml.
2	¼ cup	4 tblsp.	56 ml.
4	½ cup or¼ pint		110 ml.
5		¼pint or 1 gill	140
6	¾ cup		170
8	1 cup or ½ pint		225
9			250 (¼ l.)
10	1 ¼ cups	½ pint	280
12	1 ½ cups or ¾ pint		340
15		¾ pint	420
16	2 cups or 1 pint		450
18	2 ¼ cups		500 (½ l.)
24	3 cups or ½ pints		675
32	4 cups		900
36	4 ½ cups		1 l.

SUBSTITUTIONS AND EQUIVALENTS FOR INGREDIENTS

US - Imperial

arugula-rocket
beet-beetroot
cheesecloth-muslin
eggplant-aubergine
fresh ginger-gingeroot
scallion-spring onion
snow pea-mangetout
string bean-french bean (although French beans tend to be smaller)
zest-rind (colored part of the rind only, trim off the white pith- it tends to be bitter)
zucchini-courgettes

buttermilk- If you are making Irish soda bread or biscuits you can substitute the following for each cup of buttermilk: Stir together 1 scant cup of milk and 1 tablespoon cider vinegar. Let sit 5 minutes, then use in recipe.

heavy cream-double cream
half and half- 12% fat milk
light cream-single cream

all-purpose flour-plain (T45) flour
baking sheet- oven tray
cake flour- pastry (T55) flour
coarse salt- kitchen salt
confectioner's sugar- icing sugar
cornstarch- corn flour
granulated sugar-caster sugar
plastic wrap- cling film
unbleached flour- strong white flour
vanilla bean- vanilla pod

Acknowledgments

I would like to thank all those who have assisted me in this project:

Thank you to Gail Bellamy for her support and encouragement when this book was still notes scribbled in between rehearsals and to Spiro and Joanne Gumas for their generosity and patience when the oven broke.

A million thanks to Sean McGroarty and Annie Gaffney for their hospitality during all those weeks in London and my friend Melanie Jean-Richard for lending me her Paquita tutu.

Thank you to Marcello Angelini of Tulsa Ballet Theatre for the gracious loan of the studio and costumes and to Pat Gill and Jeannie Hahn for their talents in fitting.

I would like to applaud Tim, Jesse and Jack at F-Stop for their excellent service and superb attention to color and to Steve Pitwell and Jibak Barua for their technical help. Thanks to my mother, Joan Hymes, for her lovely tableware.

There are also many people who have helped with the testing of recipes. For their ideas, recipe testing and generous contributions in innumerable ways, I am forever grateful to: Tony Chiofolo, Alan Kluckow, Stephen Michaelides, Jenny Lester, Christopher Jean-Richard, Jeffrey and Jamie Brown, Lorna Engelman, Bill and Barbara Bock, Jaqueline Monroe and Danny Rutigliano, Preeti Vasudevan, Christopher Rankin, Craig Lee and Scott Gatz, Nettie Quackenbush, Joseph Blue Sky and Donna Webb, John and Lee Bee, Luc Vanier, Bridgie and Colin, and Noah Gelber.

And most of all, to my husband Derek, for his exceptional support and patience, and for happily reshooting pictures for no good reason- especially the ones for biscuits.

This book is dedicated to my father.